TC 3-04.72 (FM 3-04.508)
October 2009

Aviation Life Support System Management Program

Headquarters, Department of the Army

Published by Books Express Publishing
Books Express Publishing, 2011
ISBN 978-1-78039-950-8

Books Express publications are available from all good retail and online booksellers. For
publishing proposals and direct ordering please contact us at: info@books-express.com

*TC 3-04.72 (FM 3-04.508)

Training Circular No. 3-04.72 (FM 3-04.508)	Headquarters Department of the Army Washington, DC, 15 October 2009

Aviation Life Support System Management Program

Contents

DISTRIBUTION RESTRICTION: Approved for public release; distribution is unlimited.

*This publication supersedes FM 3-04.508, 23 April 2004.

Figures

Tables

Preface

Training Circular 3-04.72 provides technical information concerning Aviation Life Support System (ALSS) management and training programs. This circular is designed for commanders, their staffs, small unit leaders, and technicians who have responsibility for ALSS management. This circular supersedes Field Manual 3-04.508.

Aviation life support equipment (ALSE) enhances and sustains the safety of aircrews and passengers throughout the flight environment. ALSE incorporates comfort into items designed to provide individuals with an increased degree of survivability and recovery during an aviation mishap.

The Army prepares its Soldiers to operate anywhere in the world; this publication outlines training to assist aircrews operating in unique environments.

This publication applies to the active Army, the Army National Guard (ARNG)/Army National Guard of the United States (ARNGUS), and the United States Army Reserve (USAR) unless otherwise stated. The proponent for this publication is Headquarters, U.S. Army Training and Doctrine Command (TRADOC). Send comments and recommendations using Department of the Army Form 2028 (Recommended Changes to Publications and Blank Forms) to Commander, United States Army Aviation Center of Excellence, ATTN: ATZQ-TD-D, Fort Rucker, AL 36362-5236, or by e-mail to the Directorate of Training and Doctrine at av.doctrine@us.army.mil. Other doctrinal information can be found on the Army Knowledge Online website.

The use of trade names in this manual is for clarity only and does not constitute endorsement by the Department of Defense.

This publication has been reviewed for operations security considerations.

Chapter 1

Aviation Life Support System

This chapter provides a brief history of the developmental evolution of the Aviation Life Support System (ALSS). It also details the importance of aviation life support equipment (ALSE) to aircrews and passengers.

MANAGEMENT EVOLUTION

1-1. ALSS program management has evolved from a basic vision of establishing dedicated, safety-enhanced Army aviation equipment to a program of overarching components within a life support system. The guiding theory originally focused on ever-advancing equipment for aviators; however, it soon developed into the management of an entire system encompassing not only personal equipment but also the component systems dedicated to individual aircraft. The Air Warrior (AW) program was developed from this evolutionary process. This program includes current and future development of state-of-the-art equipment to enhance safety and provides crewmembers with situational awareness and functional yet comfortable equipment.

1-2. The AW program has long been designated by the Army as the focal point for all ALSE lifecycle management. In 1983, two organizations under direction of the Army Materiel Command—the ALSE Manager's Office and ALSE Development Team—merged to form a single office, Product Manager-Aviation Life Support Equipment (PM-ALSE). In 1996, PM-ALSE was reorganized as the Aircrew Integrated Systems (ACIS) Project Office with a mandate to validate ALSS effectiveness and ensure its full integration with mission equipment worn, carried by, or readily accessible to aviation crewmembers.

1-3. In 2000, the ACIS Project Office reverted back to a PM and was integrated into PM-Aviation Electronic Systems (PM-AES). Major accomplishments included selection of the initial AW ensemble and appointment of the PM as the primary systems integrator for the AW program.

1-4. AW program goals are to improve aircrew safety, increase aircrew and passenger survivability, and enhance aircrew performance in today's sophisticated aircraft. AW provides crewmember equipment system integration, man-machine interface, weight savings, increased survivability, and a higher potential for improved mission performance at an overall reduced cost. AW also enhances downed crewmember survivability in escape and evasion situations. In 2002, PM-AES was integrated with Program Executive Office Soldier under the control of PM-Soldier Warrior as the newly renamed AW Product Office.

EQUIPMENT EVOLUTION

1-5. AW implementation and fielding evolved in "generations" as new equipment became available. Descriptions of the first three AW generations are provided in the following paragraphs.

AIR WARRIOR GENERATION ONE

1-6. AW generation one provided an initial system capability that included the development, procurement, and fielding of:
- Flexible body armor.
- Ballistic upgrade plates.
- Primary survival gear carrier.
- First aid items.
- Universal holster.

- Aircrew survival and egress knife.
- Microclimate cooling system (including microclimate cooling garment and cooling unit).
- Overwater mission equipment (including overwater gear carrier, survival egress air, and flotation collar).

AIR WARRIOR GENERATION TWO

1-7. AW generation two technology provided additional capabilities that included the aircraft wireless intercom system and electronic data management (EDM). EDM capabilities included:

- Interface with aviation mission planning system (AMPS) and joint mission planning system.
- Moving map displays.
- Performance planning.
- Checklist/manuals.
- Use of aircraft power and global positioning system.
- Stand-alone capability for the UH-60.

Increment IV

1-8. Increment IV enhanced generation two technologies by adding the following capabilities:

- Modular integrated helmet display system with heads-up display.
- Integrated antiexposure system, laser eye protection, and chemical/biological protective gear waste management system.

AIR WARRIOR GENERATION THREE

1-9. AW generation three is the newest aircrew ensemble in the program's lifecycle. It provides advanced life support, ballistics protection, and chemical, biological, radiological, and nuclear (CBRN) protection in rapidly tailorable, mission-configurable modules. The AW concept was developed with interoperability in mind and has leveraged several joint service technology efforts. The system consists of components effectively integrated to maximize safe aircraft operation and was designed to sustain aircrews throughout the flight environment. The system increases mission effectiveness and provides a means of safe and reliable escape, survival, and recovery in emergency or combat situations. The AW generation three system is compatible with multiple airframe types including the CH-47, OH-58D, AH-64, UH-60, UH-72, C-23, and C-27J (not all AW components have been tested in these airframes). System improvements include:

- Microclimate cooling, which allows for extended flight time in mission oriented protective posture (MOPP) 4 (not compatible in the LUH-72).
- A helmet system integrated across all platforms that provides improved hearing protection, day/night helmet mounted display, advanced night vision goggles, maxillofacial shield, passive and agile laser eye protection, nuclear flash protection, and external audio.
- Hands-free wireless intercom communications between dismounted crewmembers and pilots.
- CBRN protection for all MOPP configurations.
- Water survival capabilities such as a low-profile flotation collar, integrated one-man raft, emergency underwater breathing oxygen supply, and antiexposure suit.
- Survival gear carrier fully compatible with ballistic protection body armor and provisions for the tailorable placement of personal defensive weapons and survival/egress knife.
- EDM that increases situational awareness and integrates with Blue Force Tracker on aircraft and AMPS.
- Survival radio for secure position reporting and over-the-horizon communications capability.
- Extraction harness and safety restraint integrated with survival gear carrier.
- Enhanced aircrew survivability via improved flame and chemical/biological protection.
- Hands-free breakaway connections for emergency egress.

● Equipment designed to accommodate varying threat levels and support operations in all geographical regions and environmental conditions.

This page intentionally left blank.

Chapter 2

Aviation Life Support System Management Program

The concepts and practices discussed in this chapter are guidelines for conducting the ALSS management program. Mission and operating environments may require units to modify ALSS management to support operational needs. Army aviation doctrine also affects the fielding and sustainment of ALSS maintenance operations.

Note. This TC and ATTP 3-04.7 (FM 3-04.500) provide tactics, techniques, and procedures (TTP) for aviation maintenance and are the doctrinal foundation for commanders, aviation life support equipment officers (ALSOs), aviation life support equipment noncommissioned officers (ALSNCOs), and aviation life support equipment technicians (ALSETs).

Army regulation (AR) 95-1, AR 95-20, FM 3-04 (FM 3-04.100), and ATTP 3-04.7 provide information on Army aviation structure, relationships, and command, control, and communications concepts. These publications are available on the Army Publishing Directorate's website at http://www.apd.army.mil/.

SECTION I – PROGRAM ADMINISTRATION

AVIATION LIFE SUPPORT SYSTEM

2-1. ALSS consists of the components, techniques, and training required to ensure aircrews maintain an optimal flight environment. ALSS also provides flight personnel with maximum functional capability through all environments and enhances safe and reliable escape, survival, and recovery in combat and emergency situations.

AVIATION LIFE SUPPORT SYSTEM FACILITY

2-2. ALSS facilities are established to accommodate a required number of maintenance personnel; provide maintenance areas for scheduled and unscheduled maintenance; and provide storage of ALSE, support equipment, common and special tools, repair parts, supplies, and materials. Minimum requirements for these facilities are specified in AR 95-1.

Contents

2-3. Within the ALSS facility, test equipment, tools, and pilferable ALSE components and supplies must be stored in lockable storage cabinets. Administrative areas must be established for charts, records, publications, and administrative supplies. These facilities require augmentation with a mobility capability to support unit deployment requirements.

AVIATION LIFE SUPPORT EQUIPMENT

2-4. ALSE is critical for the survivability of aviation crewmembers. Unit commanders must ensure all mission-required ALSE is available in sufficient quantities and in serviceable condition. To meet the

Army's transformation requirements, newer integrated systems that increase ALSE complexity are being fielded, a process that demands better maintenance planning and a higher degree of maintenance skill.

2-5. ALSE comforts, sustains, and protects crewmembers throughout flight and provides additional protection from impacts and postcrash fires. ALSE also enhances the means to escape, evade, and survive in combat or any hostile environment.

EQUIPMENT MAINTENANCE

Concepts and Policies

2-6. The unit's primary maintenance objective is to maintain available aircraft in mission-ready status. ALSS maintenance is critical to accomplishing missions and fulfilling other unit maintenance requirements.

2-7. Working in any type of aviation environment is challenging; however, unit ALSS programs must remain functional in all operational environments. ALSS assets are critical to sustaining communications, mobility, and survivability; maintenance of these resources should not become a secondary objective. Commanders must provide personnel and financial resourcing to effectively maintain and sustain their ALSS maintenance, training, and operational programs. Units often face critical decisions such as how to obtain required ALSE, who should perform maintenance, and how personnel should train with and use ALSE.

2-8. The following maintenance concepts and policies must be observed:
- ALSE must be maintained at mission capable status at all times.
- ALSE inspection, maintenance, and repair must be accomplished according to the applicable technical manual (TM), technical order (TO), or Naval Air (NAVAIR) publication for the equipment involved and with authorized repair parts, special tools, and test equipment.
- Unserviceable ALSE beyond the maintenance authority's capabilities must be promptly reported or delivered to the next-higher maintenance level.
- Quality maintenance depends on preventive maintenance services and inspections.
- Operator (crewmember) maintenance must be a priority and emphasized consistently throughout the chain of command. Personal maintenance is a key factor in ALSS operational readiness.
- AR 95-1, AR 95-20, and Department of the Army Pamphlet (DA Pam) 738-751 contain specific policies on ALSE use, maintenance, and responsibilities. Commanders at all levels should know and understand these policies.
- ALSE Class V items must be reviewed for stockpile reliability (surveillance) in accordance with AR 740-1, Supply Bulletin (SB) 742-1, and Technical Bulletin (TB) 9-1300-385 and recorded on DA Form 3022-R (Army Depot Surveillance Record).

Program Considerations

2-9. Major considerations for the ALSS maintenance program at field maintenance locations include—
- Maintaining the highest degree of mobility (preparing load plans and practicing deployment procedures).
- Completing all scheduled maintenance before deployment or entry into surge operations to avoid potentially unserviceable ALSE and failure to meet mission requirements.
- Setting priorities (unit commander and production control) for environmental considerations and equipment maintenance based on mission requirements.
- Managing intensive maintenance operations (this consideration is especially critical since combat operations may result in shortages of personnel, repair parts, and aircraft).
- Predesignating and training crewmembers regarding the ALSS program so minimal time and resources are expended during critical periods.

COMMANDERS

2-10. Commanders at all levels are responsible for ALSS maintenance as required in AR 95-1 and this publication. Commanders must—

- Appoint an ALSO to assist, advise, and represent the commander in all ALSS matters.
- Obtain authorized maintenance resources (for example, technically-qualified personnel, facilities, technical publications, repair parts, tools, test equipment, and maintenance supplies).
- Review required budgets and obtain funding for equipment, supplies, and repair parts to ensure a continuous and well-maintained ALSS program.
- Ensure only trained and qualified personnel maintain ALSS assets.
- Ensure ALSE is maintained in serviceable, mission-ready condition in quantities sufficient to support unit mission requirements.
- Prevent abuse of equipment under their control and investigate and act on evidence of abuse.
- Monitor Class V items for physical security and inventory and ensure explosives safety requirements are met per applicable regulations.
- Ensure aircrews perform their duties with properly inspected ALSE.
- Ensure risk management is conducted in accordance with appropriate publications.

2-11. Commanders must include ALSE maintenance and training program requirements in their budgets. They must manage funding for equipment, supplies, and repair parts to ensure continuous and well-maintained ALSE maintenance and training programs.

2-12. Commanders should resource ALSE maintenance personnel in accordance with TOE documents. One full-time ALSE maintainer should be adequate to maintain equipment for up to 50 personnel. Commanders using ALSE maintainers in a part-time capacity must adjust the number of personnel as needed to ensure all required inspections and maintenance is performed.

AVIATION LIFE SUPPORT OFFICER

2-13. In addition to the responsibilities listed in AR 95-1, ALSOs must—

- Assist, advise, and represent the commander in all matters pertaining to ALSS.
- Possess additional skill identifier (ASI) H2 (ALSO).
- Keep up-to-date standing operating procedures (SOPs) governing ALSS maintenance management and training programs (see appendix A of this publication for guidance) and ensure compliance with Army aviation maintenance and training doctrine.
- Prepare an annual ALSE budget.
- Schedule ALSS maintenance and plan, supervise, and manage unit ALSS maintenance programs.
- Develop and execute ALSS training programs to track crewmember proficiency requirements.
- Develop and execute training programs to maintain and track ALSS technician proficiency.
- Develop and execute training programs regarding proper wear and use of assigned ALSS equipment.
- Coordinate with operations officers (S3s) to determine and provide the amount and type of ALSE needed to meet mission requirements.
- Maintain inventory control records to identify locations of all ALSS shop-assigned property such as vests, radios, life preservers, and test equipment.
- Ensure authorized repair parts and maintenance supplies are available or have valid requisition.
- Ensure outstanding supply requests are accomplished promptly.
- Ensure all Class V items are physically secured and inventoried and explosives safety requirements are maintained according to applicable regulations.

AVIATION LIFE SUPPORT EQUIPMENT TECHNICIAN

2-14. In accordance with AR 95-1 and this publication, ALSETs will be appointed to assist, advise, and represent the ALSO in matters pertaining to ALSE. ALSETs must—

- Possess ASI Q2 (ALSE) and meet military occupational specialty (MOS) requirements per DA Pam 611-21 (for enlisted Soldiers).
- Perform scheduled and unscheduled maintenance on assigned ALSS equipment.
- Process ALSS test equipment for calibration and ensure shipment of ALSS equipment requiring repair at a higher maintenance level.
- Maintain a skill efficiency level sufficient to perform unassisted maintenance on and fitting of ALSS equipment.
- Coordinate higher-level maintenance for items beyond the capabilities of the ALSE shop due to a lack of skills, tools, or test equipment.
- Replace unserviceable end-item equipment components.
- Record the receipt, operation, maintenance, calibration, modification, and transfer of equipment.
- Maintain a publication library to ensure compliance with administration, maintenance, physical security, supply, and explosives safety regulations and procedures.

AIRCREWS

2-15. Crew members must—

- Use equipment properly.
- Keep equipment clean, presentable, safe, and operable.
- Report any malfunction beyond their capabilities or authorization to correct.
- Perform maintenance and inspections before, during, and after operations per unit SOP and applicable TMs.
- Be accountable for assigned equipment.

SECTION III – BUDGET MANAGEMENT

COMMANDER'S RESPONSIBILITY AND BUDGET PROCESS

2-16. The following steps (paragraphs 2-16 through 2-19) allow commanders to develop initial ALSE cost analyses or identify equipment shortages for forecasting annual budgets and future requirements. To obtain repair parts and figure maintenance supply costs, commanders must use the proper maintenance shop stock, operational load, and prescribed load list (PLL) procedures listed in AR 710-2, DA Pam 710-2-1, and DA Pam 710-2-2. Other factors to consider when determining maintenance budgets include unit mission, training requirements, and unscheduled maintenance contingencies. ALSS personnel must maintain records outlining the steps and equipment authorizations used to figure budget requests.

STEP ONE: DETERMINE PERSONNEL AUTHORIZATIONS

2-17. Some ALSE authorizations (such as helmets, vests, survival radios, survival kits, and oxygen masks) are based on the unit's authorized number of crew members and non-crew members. Common Table of Allowances (CTA) 50-900, AR 95-1, tables of distribution and allowances (TDAs), and modification tables of organization and equipment (MTOEs) specify equipment authorizations. ALSOs and ALSETs should refer to their unit's TDA and MTOE to determine crew and non-crew authorizations and orders.

STEP TWO: DETERMINE AIRCRAFT AUTHORIZATIONS

2-18. Some ALSE (such as life rafts and first aid and survival kits) are based on aircraft type, seat availability, and unit mission. CTA 8-100, CTA 50-900, AR 95-1, and aircraft operator's manuals specify equipment authorizations. ALSOs and ALSETs should refer to their unit's TDA and MTOE to determine mission statement, number and type of aircraft authorizations, and proper aircraft operator's manual.

STEP THREE: DETERMINE EQUIPMENT AUTHORIZATIONS

2-19. Various ARs, CTAs, SBs, MTOEs, and TDAs authorize unit ALSE. ALSOs and ALSETs should maintain a list of required and authorized equipment based on appropriate publications and unit mission.

STEP FOUR: DETERMINE ON-HAND QUANTITIES

2-20. To determine on-hand quantities, ALSS personnel must conduct a 100-percent inventory of unit ALSE and list each piece in a locally produced document. All authorized equipment is accounted for if the numbers are equal. If the on-hand quantity is greater than that authorized, the overage must be noted in the remarks column. If the on-hand quantity is less than that authorized, the on-hand number must be subtracted from the authorized number and any shortages noted in the remarks column. Shortage lists are used to determine annual budgets by referencing the proper supply publications for obtaining cost and equipment data. A sample budgeting and maintenance scheduling process is provided in table 2-1.

Table 2-1. Sample budgeting and maintenance scheduling process

1. Personnel authorizations (TDA and MTOE)			Cumulative
	Officers	Enlisted	Total
Crew members	30	15	45
Non-crew members	0	3	3
Total	30	18	48
2. Aircraft authorizations (TDA and MTOE)			
	Total Number	Type Aircraft	Seat Availability
	15	UH-60	210 (14 per aircraft)
3. Determine equipment authorizations			
4. Equipment authorizations (ARs, CTAs, SBs, TDA, MTOE) and on-hand quantities (inventory)			
	Authorized	On Hand	Remarks
Helmet	48	58	Overage 10
Life preserver	258	210	Shortage 48
Life raft, 7-man	30	24	Shortage 6
Mask, oxygen	45	45	
Radio, survival	45	35	Shortage 10
	Authorized	On Hand	Remarks
Survival kit, individual, cold climate	45	42	Shortage 3
Survival kit, individual, hot climate	45	42	Shortage 3
Survival kit, individual, overwater	45	42	Shortage 3
Vest, body armor	48	48	
Vest, survival	48	48	
Total	657	594	Shortage 73 (get-well budget)
5. Daily inspection requirements			
Authorized: 657 divided by 84 = 7.8 or 8 On Hand: 584 divided by 84 = 6.9 or 7			
6. Establish realistic inspection team criteria			
7. Schedule/manage equipment inspections			

SECTION IV – MAINTENANCE

PROGRAM MANAGEMENT

2-21. Both aviation and ALSE maintenance is performed on a 24-hour basis. The guiding concept is to "replace forward-repair rear" so units can return aircraft and crews to meet immediate operational needs.

2-22. ALSE-qualified personnel currently on orders are responsible for ALSE maintenance beyond the capabilities or responsibilities of crew members. ALSE personnel must conduct the following maintenance tasks:

- Scheduled periodic maintenance inspections and repair of ALSE items.
- Unscheduled maintenance of ALSE items that fail preflight inspection or are identified as unserviceable by crew members.
- Scheduled periodic maintenance inspections and repair of operational and training ALSE items.

SCHEDULING

2-23. Scheduled ALSE maintenance is necessary to preserve high maintenance standards. Constant coordination between the S3, ALSO, and ALSET is required to balance mission requirements with adequate maintenance time.

COORDINATION

2-24. To properly schedule ALSE maintenance, the ALSO or ALSET must have vital information regarding unit mission, aircraft, personnel, and equipment authorizations. Maintaining proper documentation and effectively coordinating between maintenance elements is vital in ensuring serviceable ALSE is available for unit use. By completing the following steps, the ALSO will assist in providing this information to ALSS personnel. Once completed, the scheduling process may be used for budgeting and maintenance scheduling.

2-25. The supporting quality assurance specialist (ammunition surveillance) (QASAS) representative must schedule required annual inspections for Class V items. Daily surveillance checks must be completed according to AR 702-6, AR 740-1, DA Pam 385-64, and SB 742-1.

SCHEDULING PROCESS

2-26. The following steps outline the maintenance scheduling process. The four steps described in paragraphs 2-16 through 2-19 should be repeated sequentially for this process.

STEP FIVE: DETERMINE DAILY INSPECTION REQUIREMENTS

2-27. After completing steps three and four (paragraphs 2-18 and 2-19), the ALSO or ALSET should divide personnel and equipment totals by the inspection cycle to determine daily inspection requirements. For example, there are three 120-day inspection cycles per year; on average, there are an estimated 84 working days in a 120-day cycle. With this information, the following formulas may be used to determine daily inspection requirements:

- Total equipment authorized divided by 84 equals daily inspection requirements (authorization).
- Total equipment on hand divided by 84 equals daily inspection requirements (real world).

STEP SIX: ESTABLISH REALISTIC INSPECTION ITEM CRITERIA

2-28. ALSOs and ALSETs must determine the time required to perform periodic inspections on ALSS assets. Maintenance allocation charts (MACs) listed in equipment maintenance manuals provide a guide for appropriate inspection times. Times listed are for conduct of inspections only and do not allow for performing repairs or maintenance, completing forms and records, or ordering parts. ALSS personnel and supervisors must consider and compensate for these tasks during scheduling. Other factors include working hours and conditions, physical training programs, formations, duty rosters, shop equipment maintenance, and unscheduled ALSE maintenance.

STEP SEVEN: SCHEDULE AND MANAGE EQUIPMENT INSPECTIONS

2-29. ALSS personnel must evaluate the time allotted to perform ALSE maintenance before unit equipment inspections can be scheduled and managed. In addition, they must regulate inspection intervals to prevent an unmanageable workload and critical ALSE shortage. The goal is for ALSS maintenance to flow smoothly by spreading inspections throughout a given cycle rather than forcing them into 1 or 2 months. Coordination with operations is vital to ensuring ALSE is available to meet all mission requirements, including temporary duties and field exercises.

AUTOMATION

2-30. Several methods are available for tracking inspection requirements and maintaining ALSE accountability (it is important to note, however, that shops must standardize equipment tracking methods within their respective groups). Many ALSETs have developed spreadsheets to track required inspection information. This and other methods used by ALSETs are permissible if they meet U.S. Army Forces Command (FORSCOM) aviation resource management survey (ARMS) checklist requirements. In addition, two software programs—Tracker 2.0 and the Automated Life Support Management System—are available to assist ALSETs in meeting accountability requirements.

Tracker 2.0

2-31. Tracker 2.0 was developed to assist ALSE maintainers in managing their maintenance programs. Additional information on this software is available at https://airwarrior.redstone.army.mil/default.asp.

Automated Life Support Management System

2-32. The Automated Life Support Management System (ALSMS) is a tool authorized for use by ALSE personnel to best meet the unit's program management needs. Units tracking equipment with ALSMS are not required to duplicate information on a status board or in a card catalog; all that is needed is a system-generated computer printout.

2-33. ALSMS is a free program available for download at http://armyalsms.com. When installed, the program downloads a user manual to the computer's hard drive. This manual is written at the beginner's level and has a "what's new" section for advanced users.

2-34. ALSMS may be installed as a stand-alone computer system or set up as a shared database where several computers have access to the same data. The user manual explains how to install the program on multiple systems and share databases across a local area network.

INSPECTIONS

2-35. Commanders and ALSS program managers must ensure their maintenance programs provide the assets aircrews need without compromising established, safe maintenance standards. ALSE maintenance personnel and crew members must perform different types of inspections to maintain assigned ALSE.

PREVENTIVE MAINTENANCE CHECKS AND SERVICES

2-36. Individual crewmembers must perform preventive maintenance checks and services (PMCS), which includes proper care and cleaning of equipment such as flight clothing and helmets. ALSS personnel must perform PMCS per the appropriate TM and establish inspections at prescribed intervals.

Preflight Inspections

2-37. Individual crew members must perform preflight inspections prior to flight; no special technical skills are required. Crewmembers must verify ALSE items are in serviceable condition, ensure inspection dates are current, and report any discrepancies to qualified ALSE personnel.

Postflight Inspections

2-38. Individual crew members must conduct postflight inspections after each flight and notify ALSE personnel of any discrepancies.

SPECIAL INSPECTIONS

2-39. ALSE personnel must perform special inspections whenever conditions warrant. The inspector or directive determines the extent of these inspections, which usually are conducted per the appropriate TM. For example, equipment should be inspected after exposure to dusty environments, CBRN agents, or other contaminants.

INITIAL ACCEPTANCE INSPECTIONS

2-40. ALSE personnel must inspect all newly acquired equipment to ensure serviceability and validate serial numbers. They also must inspect shipments to ensure all ordered components were received.

TURN-IN INSPECTIONS

2-41. ALSE personnel must inspect equipment and clothing to be turned in to supply shops or central issue facilities (CIFs). These inspections include properly identifying equipment serviceability and labeling items with appropriate materiel condition tags.

SERVICEABLE PARTS INSPECTIONS

2-42. ALSE personnel must perform serviceable parts inspections to determine whether parts removed from unserviceable equipment such as helmets, life preservers, and oxygen masks are serviceable.

COMMAND INSPECTIONS

2-43. Commanders and staff personnel must conduct formal and informal command inspections to determine equipment reliability and performance and gauge maintenance program effectiveness. Command inspections include periodic visits by an aviation safety officer (ASO) and completion of aviation accident prevention surveys. The flight surgeon should monitor ALSS operations and assist in training the physiological and medical aspects of survival, as well as the fitting and use of ALSE by aircrew personnel. Commanders and ALSE personnel should use the FORSCOM ARMS checklist, available on the Army Knowledge Online website at https://www.us.army.mil/suite/page/592726, when conducting these inspections.

QUALITY ASSURANCE SPECIALIST (AMMUNITION SURVEILLANCE) INSPECTIONS

2-44. Each installation, activity, and command must establish and maintain a QASAS program in accordance with AR 702-6, AR 740-1, DA Pam 385-64, and SB 742-1.

GRAPHICS DISPLAYS

2-45. Status boards and inspection calendars are graphical tools that display data concerning ALSE status or shop operations. Although maintenance managers may have quick access to information through automation, well-planned and informative status boards and inspection calendars are highly visible information sources for commanders and other essential personnel.

STATUS BOARD

2-46. There are several methods for marking and identifying ALSE; however, what suits one unit may not be useful for another. One method for controlling and managing maintenance inspection programs is the ALSE status board (table 2-2). Information recorded on these boards is used to control current operations and plan and measure work performed. However, a status board is only as good as the information it contains; it must be current and accurate.

Table 2-2. Sample ALSE status board

Name	#	Helmet	Vest	Oxygen Mask	#	Survival Radio	Cold Kit	Hot Kit	Overwater Kit	Antiexposure Suits	First Aid Kits	7-Man Life Rafts	Life Preservers
MAJ Frank	1	FEB	FEB	FEB	1	MAR	store	JUN	MAR	FEB	FEB	store	MAR
CPT Jack	2	JAN	JAN	JAN	2	APR	JAN	JUL	APR	JAN	JAN	APR	APR
CPT Baker	3	APR	APR	APR	3	MAY	MAR	FEB	MAY	MAR	APR	MAY	MAY
CPT Snow	4	MAR	MAR	MAR	4	AUG	MAR	JAN	AUG	MAR	MAR	AUG	AUG
CW4 Solo	5	FEB	FEB	FEB	5	SEP	APR	APR	SEP	APR	FEB	SEP	SEP
CW4 Tom	6	OCT	OCT	OCT	6	NOV	FEB	APR	NOV	FEB	OCT	NOV	NOV
CW3 Ash	7	APR	APR	APR	7	JAN	MAR	JUL	JAN	MAR	APR	JAN	JAN
CW3 Bars	8	JUN	JUN	JUN	8	OCT	FEB	AUG	OCT	FEB	JUN	JAN	JAN
CW2 Taos	9	AUG	AUG	AUG	9	MAY	FEB	DEC	MAY	FEB	AUG	MAY	MAY
CW2 Sand	10	OCT	OCT	OCT	10	JUL	OCT	store	JUL	OCT	OCT	JUL	JUL
SFC Kurt	11	DEC	DEC	DEC	11	FEB	NOV	DEC	FEB	NOV	DEC	FEB	FEB
SGT Smith	12	APR	APR	APR	12	NOV	NOV	OCT	NOV	NOV	APR	store	NOV

INSPECTION CALENDAR

2-47. The sample inspection calendar located in appendix C of this manual provides a quick reference for inspections and inspection due dates. A copy of this calendar should be located near the ALSE status board for easy access. The calendar includes 90-, 120-, 180-, and 360-day inspection intervals.

LOGISTICS AND MAINTENANCE ASSISTANCE

2-48. The U.S. Army Aviation and Missile Command (AMCOM), U.S. Army Combat Readiness/Safety Center (USACRC), U.S. Army Aviation Center of Excellence, and U.S. Army Aviation Logistics School are source agencies from which general and specific ALSE materials may be obtained.

PRODUCT MANAGER-AIR WARRIOR

2-49. PM-AW's vision statement is to "design, develop, and produce aircrew products that provide exceptional warfighting effectiveness, unparalleled mission versatility, increased aircraft lethality, and unmatched survivability while both sustainable and affordable. To have these products available becomes the choice of combat aircrews Department of Defense (DOD)-wide."

2-50. PM-AW's mission statement is to "lead and build responsible, caring, and accountable government and contractor integrated product and process teams who safely design, develop, and produce the next generation of aircrew related warfighting systems and life support equipment for Army and DOD warfighters that save lives, enhance crew performance, and are combat effective, affordable, and sustainable worldwide."

2-51. PM-AW may be contacted by mail at AMCOM, PM-AW, SFAE-SDR-AW, Redstone Arsenal, AL 35898-5000; by telephone at (256) 876-4703, DSN 746-4703, or FAX (256) 313-4946; or online at https://airwarrior.redstone.army.mil. The AW website is a valuable resource for ALSE information; it is recommended that all ALSE shops have access to the site (user identification and a password are required).

AVIATION RESOURCE MANAGEMENT SURVEY

2-52. The ARMS is a FORSCOM program designed to provide aviation personnel with expert technical assistance and onsite evaluations as mandated by AR 95-1. Additional information, assistance, and the ARMS commander's guide may be found online at https://www.us.army.mil/suite/page/592726. Key ARMS proponent areas include, but are not limited to, the following:

- Maintenance.
- Supply.
- Safety (command support programs).
- Petroleum, oil, and lubricants (POL).
- ALSE.
- Operations.
- Aviation medicine.
- Standardization.
- Training management.

SECTION V – REFERENCE MATERIALS AND ADMINISTRATIVE MANAGEMENT

REFERENCE LIBRARY

2-53. Reference libraries must contain publications required to effectively manage unit ALSS maintenance management and training programs. Required publications include the following:

- ARs.
- TMs.
- FMs.
- CTAs.
- SBs.
- TOs.
- NAVAIR publications.
- TBs.
- Supply catalogs.
- Modification work orders (MWOs).
- Safety of flight/aviation safety action messages.

2-54. The following related publications should be included in the unit reference library:
- Available ALSE/safety publications from other services.
- Professional Bulletin-1 series, *The United States Army Aviation Digest* (1955-1995).
- TB 43-postscript-557, *The Preventive Maintenance Monthly*.
- *Flightfax* and *Knowledge* magazines.
- ALSE pamphlets and bulletins.

TECHNICAL LIBRARY

2-55. ALSS shop technical files and libraries are required for all equipment; therefore, ALSOs must ensure publications subaccounts are established with the organization's publications manager. Publications must be readily available for reference and internal and external inspections.

MAINTENANCE LIBRARY UPDATE

2-56. Periodically, but not less than quarterly, publications files must be inspected to ensure complete, current publications are in use. DA Pam 25-30 governs publications maintenance and contains the following information:
- Blank forms.
- Forms and publications (new, revised, changed, superseded, rescinded, and obsolete).
- Administrative publications.
- Manuals (doctrinal and training).
- Cross-references (alphabetic, national stock number [NSN], and line item number [LIN]).
- Publications control officers.
- Installation publications control officers.
- Forms management officers (major commands).
- TMs.

PUBLICATIONS AGENCIES

2-57. There are four official Army publications agencies and one joint publication (JP) source from which ALSS personnel may obtain publications and forms online:
- Army Publishing Directorate, http://www.apd.army.mil.
- General Dennis J. Reimer Training and Doctrine Digital Library, http://www.adtdl.army.mil.
- U.S. Army Logistics Support Activity (LOGSA), http://www.logsa.army.mil.
- U.S. Army Medical Department, http://www.armymedicine.army.mil.
- Joint Electronic Library, http://www.dtic.mil/doctrine/index.htm.

CHANGED, REVISED, OR RESCINDED PUBLICATIONS

2-58. Effective ALSE maintenance requires the latest technical information be available at all times. ALSS personnel must ensure the ALSS shop has adequate quantities of current publications. Publications are continually updated; therefore, it is necessary to understand how the publications distribution system operates. DA Pam 25-40 provides information on posting and filing publications. DA Pam 25-33 explains the following:
- How initial distribution and resupply are made.
- Which DA forms are required to order publications.
- Where to order publications.
- How a publications account is set up.

INTERSERVICE PUBLICATIONS ACCOUNTS

U.S. Air Force Publications

2-59. U.S. Air Force publications may be obtained online at https://www.my.af.mil/faf/FAF/fafHome.jsp. Once a user establishes an account, he or she may access the technical order viewing library, which contains publications in electronic format.

U.S. Navy Publications

2-60. U.S. Navy publications may be viewed digitally or paper copies requested at https://mynatec navair.navy.mil/. Users must request a new user account to access or request publications.

MAINTENANCE MANAGEMENT FILES

2-61. As with any maintenance function, certain files must be maintained in accordance with the Army Record Information Management System, AR 25-400-2, and local command policies. Files should consist of, but are not limited to, the following:

- Equipment improvement recommendations (EIRs).
- Product quality deficiency reports.
- Report of discrepancy form (Standard Form [SF] 364).
- Command directives.
- Inspections/surveys.
- Correspondence.
- Council meetings.
- Orders.
- Bulletins.
- Suspense files.
- Facsimile files.
- Maintenance records (per DA Pam 738-751).
- DA Form 2028.
- Budget files.
- Supply files.
- Training files.

ELECTRONIC PUBLICATIONS

2-62. The DOD objective is to automate all reference and administrative publications and documents into electronic format. ALSS personnel should utilize electronic technical manuals (ETMs), interactive ETMs, and other electronic publications and documents.

SECTION VI – EQUIPMENT ACCOUNTABILITY, RESPONSIBILITY, AND CONTROL

ACCOUNTABILITY AND RESPONSIBILITY

2-63. Property accountability is one of the greatest challenges facing company commanders, ALSOs, and ALSETs. Commanders are responsible for keeping the unit's property in serviceable condition. They must emphasize that each person is responsible for all property in his or her charge, including items not listed in unit property books. Commanders also must ensure their Soldiers account for unit property. AR 710-2 and AR 735-5 contain Army policy for property accountability and responsibility. DA Pam 710-2-1 contains manual procedures for property accountability.

AMMUNITION AND EXPLOSIVES CONTROL

2-64. Commanders are responsible for controlling ammunition and explosives and other sensitive items within their units. AR 710-2 requires inventory for sensitive and Class V items. ALSE sensitive and Class V items are inventoried by quantity, lot number, and serial number (if applicable). After inventory is complete, the commander must sign a statement reflecting inventory results. For units without a property book, a copy of the inventory must be maintained and the original forwarded to the property book officer (PBO). Ammunition and explosives storage must be in accordance with AR 190-11, SOPs, and local directives.

LOCK AND KEY CONTROL

2-65. AR 190-11 and AR 190-13 explain measures for lock and key control. Local physical security officers can assist in ensuring standards are met. A lock and key custodian must be appointed to ensure all unit keys and locks are handled properly. The lock and key custodian must maintain a record of locks and keys used by ALSS personnel on DA Form 5513-R (Key Control Register and Inventory). AR 190-11 provides regulatory guidance for completion of DA Form 5513-R.

ACCOUNTABILITY AND CONTROL SPECIFIC TO AVIATION LIFE SUPPORT EQUIPMENT

2-66. ALSS personnel should possess and use the following publications to complete property accountability and control forms and records. They also should use these publications to become familiar with property accountability and security policies and procedures.

DEPARTMENT OF THE ARMY PAMPHLET 710-2-1 AND DEPARTMENT OF THE ARMY PAMPHLET 710-2-2

2-67. DA Pam 710-2-1 and DA Pam 710-2-2 provide detailed information on inspection and inventory procedures. Receipt and issue of property inventory, changes in responsible officer inventory, and annual responsible officer or cyclic inventory methods also are included. These publications also contain samples and instructions for completing the following forms:

- DA Form 2062 for hand and subhand receipt procedures.
- DA Form 3161 and Department of Defense (DD) Form 1150 for temporary hand receipts or change documents (issue or turn-in transactions).
- DA Form 3749 for equipment receipt procedures.

ARMY REGULATION 735-5

2-68. AR 735-5 contains vital information regarding accountability and responsibility. Accountability is a person's obligation to maintain accurate formal records. Responsibility is a basic obligation for the proper custody, care, use, and safekeeping of Government property. There are four types of interrelated responsibility: command, supervisory, direct, and personal. AR 735-5 also defines three types of property—nonexpendable, expendable, and durable—and covers accounting procedures for each type. If ALSS personnel experience loss of or damage to property in their care, AR 735-5 has information on methods for obtaining relief from responsibility through several systems.

OTHER IMPORTANT ARMY REGULATIONS

2-69. In addition to the publications listed above, ALSS personnel should have the following publications available for reference:

- AR 190-11. This publication provides information regarding the physical security of arms, ammunition, and explosives.
- AR 190-51. This publication provides information on marking Army property and securing storage structures, including the use of keys, locks, and chains.

● AR 710-2. This publication prescribes policy for supply operations below the wholesale level and is applicable in times of peace or war.

2-70. The ALSO, ALSNCO, or ALSET should maintain positive control of all ALSE items for inspection purposes. Local CIFs or supply facilities may issue, exchange, or control certain ALSE items. However, there must be a closed-loop system between these facilities and the ALSS shop to ensure equipment remains fully functional and conditions are accurately identified. The ALSS supervisor might need to discuss policies and procedures with these facilities to ensure condemned equipment is not reissued as serviceable. These facilities should not accept an ALSE item for turn-in or exchange unless it is tagged and signed by the ALSO, ALSNCO, or ALSET in accordance with DA Pam 738-751. In addition, exchanged or issued ALSE items must be taken to the ALSS shop for proper inspection prior to use. The unit ALSS SOP must contain specific policies and procedures regarding CIF-issued items.

SECTION VII – DEPLOYMENT PLAN

2-71. This section assists ALSS personnel in preparing and supporting units deployed by land, sea, or air. Deployments usually are divided into four phases: preparation, movement to the port of embarkation, actions at the port of embarkation, and actions at the port of debarkation. The following publications must be available for reference:

● AR 220-10.
● FM 55-9.
● FM 55-12.
● FM 55-30.
● FM 55-65.
● FORSCOM Regulation 55-1.
● FORSCOM Regulation 55-2.
● TB 55-46-1.
● TM 1-1500-344-23.
● TM 38-250.
● TM 55-1520-400-14.

PREPARATION

2-72. Commanders and ALSS personnel should take the following steps to prepare their units for deployment:

● Review ALSS maintenance and historical records for upcoming services, inspections, component replacements, or deferred maintenance that might affect the unit's anticipated missions.
● Identify shortages in all classes of supply, order-replenishment quantities, and additional sustainment needs (parts might not be available at the deployed location).
● Coordinate priority assistance from test, measurement, and diagnostic equipment (TMDE) support facilities for calibration requirements.
● Ensure vehicle load plans have space for mission-essential equipment using standardized load cards.
● Ensure all property book items are listed on DD Form 1750 (Packing List) by LIN and serial number.
● Determine transportation requirements beyond organic capabilities.

2-73. In addition to the steps listed above, self-deployment of aviation assets requires extended maintenance efforts during preparation and execution. To better support self-deployment, maintenance operations should consider and plan for the following:

● Not all the unit's aircraft and crews may be deployed. Aircraft used to perform missions at homestation will require routine maintenance. Support may be required to meet both the deployed and homestation components' missions.

- Maintenance personnel may be required to perform primary duties as mechanics, component repairers, supply technicians, or inspectors, as well as additional duties as door gunners.
- Support services might not be established in the theater of operations for several weeks. Sufficient amounts of required supply classes, adequate TMDE, aviation ground support equipment, special tools, and repair parts may not be available immediately.

SECTION VIII – AVIATION LIFE SUPPORT EQUIPMENT RETRIEVAL PROGRAM

2-74. When an accident or mishap occurs, an investigator is responsible for analyzing how well the logistics support element (LSE) or other protective clothing and equipment (PCE) performed their respective jobs. If the investigator finds equipment did not operate as designed, he or she must further determine whether the item contributed to or caused injury.

2-75. All LSE and PCE that is in any way implicated in the cause or prevention of injury will be recorded in the accident report. Air and ground items that caused injury, failed to function as designed, or were significant in preventing injury should be shipped to the U.S. Army Aeromedical Research Laboratory (USAARL) for further analysis. This equipment includes, but is not limited to, helmets, survival vests and components, body armor, crashworthy seat systems, restraint harnesses, inertial reels, seat belts, and air bags

2-76. Personnel with questions regarding which items should be shipped and what supporting documentation is required should contact USAARL at (334) 255-6960/6805/6893 or DSN 558-6960/6805/6893. Before the field investigation is complete, the investigation board president will arrange for shipment of equipment to: Commander, USAARL, ATTN: Crew Injury/Life Support Equipment Branch, Building 6901, P.O. Box 620577, Fort Rucker, AL 36362-0577. Equipment sent to USAARL for laboratory analysis must be noted on DA Form 2397 (Technical Report of U.S. Army Aircraft Accident). The user/wearer of each LSE/PCE item must be identified; items with multiple components (such as survival vests) should be counted as one item unless a component was separated from the item during the accident sequence. When analysis is complete, USAARL will dispose of unserviceable items and return serviceable equipment to the unit of origin or supply system.

2-77. Upon request by the USACRC, a copy of the completed laboratory analysis must be furnished for inclusion in the final accident report.

2-78. DA Pam 385-40 covers in detail the Aviation Life Support Equipment Retrieval Program (ALSERP).

This page intentionally left blank.

Chapter 3

Supply and Materiel Management

This chapter covers supply and materiel operations required for sustainment of unit ALSS maintenance management and training programs. The Army's current ALSS inventory includes items from the Army, Air Force, and Navy. ALSS personnel must understand basic supply procedures to assist supply personnel in obtaining equipment and maintaining supplies required to support day-to-day functions. Commanders must ensure ALSS supply procedures are outlined in the unit SOP. Since most of the information needed for procuring ALSE is on CD-ROM (Electronic Manual 00021), ALSS personnel must have available, or have direct access to, a computer capable of reading compact discs. AR 710-2, DA Pam 710-2-1, and DA Pam 710-2-2 address supply procedures and policies.

SECTION I – SUPPLY PUBLICATIONS AND FORMS

INFORMATION SOURCES

3-1. Certain information sources are required for ALSS personnel to provide supply personnel with correct and updated information. The following information sources may be accessed online at http://dlis.dla.mil/govord.htm:

Contents

- The Federal logistics (FEDLOG) database—
  - Lists cross-referenced NSNs, reference numbers, part numbers, and commercial and Government entity (CAGE) codes.
  - Lists reference numbers and CAGE codes in alphanumeric sequence.
  - Lists NSNs in national item identification number sequence.
  - Contains the Army Master Data File (AMDF). Published monthly, the AMDF is the official source of current supply management data for items managed or used by the Army.
  - Is published quarterly on CD-ROM.
- The universal data repository (UDR)—
  - Identifies medical and dental items essential for addressing wartime medical issues.
  - Assists the medical and dental industries in satisfying war surge and sustaining medical materiel requirements.
  - Is a subscription-only service. ALSS personnel must contact the UDR via e-mail (dlis-cso@dlis.dla.mil for active and Reserve components; udrsubscriptions@ngb.army.mil or medcatsubscriptions@ngb.army.mil for National Guard components) to request a subscription.

3-2. The following publications provide data and guidance regarding logistical procedures:

- AR 30-18 provides procedures to manage Class I supplies.
- AR 40-61 provides policy and procedures for Class VIII medical supplies.
- AR 190-11 provides physical security guidance for ammunition and explosives.
- AR 190-51 prescribes policies, procedures, and responsibilities for safeguarding unclassified Army property (sensitive and nonsensitive).
- AR 702-6 establishes policy and responsibilities, including demilitarization, for monitoring the performance, reliability, and safety characteristics of ammunition items and Class V components.

3-3. The following programs apply to conventional and chemical ammunition, small and large rockets, and guided missile ammunition and materiel:

- AR 710-1 prescribes uniform policies and procedures, guidance, and responsibilities for the development, preparation, publication, and maintenance of storage standards for materiel managed by the DOD, Government service agencies, and Coast Guard.
- AR 710-2 provides Army-wide supply policy below the wholesale level, as well as specific policy for establishing bench stock, shop stock, PLL, and operational loads.
- AR 735-5 provides policy and procedures for property accountability.
- AR 740-1 prescribes policy and procedures for the formation and management of materiel storage and supply operations.
- CTAs prescribe allowances for clothing and equipment (CTA 50-900), field and garrison furnishings and equipment (CTA 50-909), and medical items (CTA 8-100).
- DA Pam 710-2-1 provides manual procedures for requesting, receiving, issuing, accounting for, and turning in supplies, as well as guidance for establishing and maintaining PLLs.
- DA Pam 710-2-2 provides manual procedures for establishing and maintaining shop stock and bench stock at the support maintenance level, as well as guidance for establishing and maintaining shop stock procedures.
- SB 708-48 contains two sections used for cross-referencing CAGE codes and manufacturers' names and addresses. Section A is name to code and section B is code to name. SB 708-48 is published every 2 months on microfiche.
- SB 742-1 provides procedures to implement DA ammunition surveillance policies established in AR 702-6 and describes functions of the DA ammunition surveillance program as defined in AR 740-1.
- SCs provide data for identifying and managing items used by the Army.
- TB 9-1300-385 applies to all DA activities with mission responsibility and lists storage, issue, use, test, maintenance, and transportation of Class V materiel (to include restricted and suspended munitions) managed by the U.S. Army Operations Support Command and AMCOM.

FORMS

3-4. ALSS personnel must coordinate with their supply shops to complete the following forms (see DA Pam 710-2-1, DA Pam 750-8, and DA Pam 738-751 for use, preparation, and disposition):

- DA Form 581 (Request for Issue and Turn-In of Ammunition) and DA Form 581-1 (Request for Issue and Turn-In of Ammunition Continuation Sheet) are available electronically on the Army Publishing Directorate's website, http://www.apd.army.mil/.
- DA Form 2062 (Hand Receipt/Annex Number) is used to record issue of nonexpendable and durable items (Army requirements code "nonexpendable" and "durable").
- DA Form 2064 (Document Register for Supply Actions) allows personnel to record supply transactions. Quantities requested, received, adjusted, turned in, or due in are entered on one of three types of document registers: nonexpendable, durable, and expendable.

- DA Form 2765-1 (Request for Issue or Turn-In) is used to request expendable, durable, or nonexpendable single line items with NSNs listed in the AMDF (FEDLOG). It is also used to turn in all property except Class V items.
- DA Form 3161 (Request for Issue or Turn-In) is used to record issue and turn-in transactions between the PBO, hand receipt holder, and subhand receipt holder. DD Form 1150 (Request for Issue or Turn-in) and DD Form 1348-1A (Issue Release/Receipt Document) may be used in lieu of DA Form 3161 as a change document if local procedures permit.
- DD Form 1348-6 (DOD Single Line Item Requisition System Document) is used to request non-NSN single line items, NSN single line items not listed in the AMDF (FEDLOG), MWO and modification kits, classified items, and all exceptional data requests. Completion of DD Form 1348-6 is almost always mandatory for Air Force or Navy items not listed in the AMDF or those requiring exceptional data.
- DD Form 448 (Military Interdepartmental Purchase Request) is used by installation and command supply shops to support DA Form 2765-1 or DD Form 1348-6. DD Form 448 may be required for items such as life rafts and oxygen testers obtained from the Air Force or Navy.
- SF 364 (Report of Discrepancy) is used by ALSE personnel when supplies are defective or damaged due to shipping or packaging. AR 735-11-2 covers the preparation, use, and disposition of SF 364.
- SF 368 (Product Quality Deficiency Report) is completed and submitted by ALSE personnel when received items, parts, or components display a manufacturer deficiency or error. DA Pam 738-751 covers the preparation, use, and disposition of SF 368.
- SF 368 is also used to make equipment improvement recommendations (EIRs) to improve equipment performance and maintenance. Personnel preparing an SF 368 for use as an EIR should check AR 672-20 for provisions regarding suggested improvements and monetary incentives. DA Pam 738-751 covers the preparation, use, and disposition of SF 368.

SECTION II – SUPPLY PROCEDURES

SUPPLY CLASSES

3-5.   Table 3-1 provides definitions and examples of the 10 supply classes.

Table 3-1. Supply classes

Class	Definition
Class I	Subsistence items and gratuitous health and welfare items (B-rations, meals ready to eat, and fresh fruits and vegetables)
Class II	Equipment other than principal items prescribed in authorization and allowance tables (individual equipment, clothing, tentage, tool sets, and administrative supplies)
Class III	POL, further defined as packaged and bulk POL; Class III (packaged) includes hydraulic and insulating oils, chemical products, antifreeze compounds, and compressed gases; Class III (bulk) includes multifuels and gasoline
Class IV	Construction and barrier materials (lumber, sandbags, and barbed wire)
Class V	Ammunition such as small arms, artillery projectiles, antitank missiles, explosives, mines, bombs, and special ammunition such as chemical and nuclear munitions
Class VI	Personal demand items normally purchased through the exchange system (such as candy and cigarettes); Class VI items are normally requisitioned and distributed with Class I items
Class VII	Major end items (vehicles, self-propelled artillery pieces, missile launchers, aircraft, and major weapons systems)
Class VIII	Medical materiel (medicine, stretchers, surgical instruments, and medical equipment repair parts)
Class IX	Repair parts and components (kits and assemblies) and items required for support of all equipment (batteries, spark plugs, and fuel lines)
Class X	Materiel required to support civil affairs operations (such as commercial design tractors for use by local civilians)

AUTHORIZED REPAIR PARTS STOCKAGE

BENCH STOCK

3-6.   Bench stocks consist of low-cost, high-use, consumable Class II, Class III (packaged), Class IV, and Class IX (fewer components) items. Examples include common hardware, resistors, transistors, capacitors, wire, tubing, hoses, ropes, webbing, thread, welding rods, sandpaper, gasket materiel, sheet metal, seals, oils, grease, and repair kits. AR 710-2 lists the criteria an item must meet to qualify as bench stock. ALSOs or maintenance officers must approve bench stock lists semiannually.

3-7.   Bench stocks are not demand supported; units do not need a certain number of demands for an item to remain on bench stock. Maintenance activities with a collocated supply support activity (SSA) maintain a 15-day supply of bench stock; activities without a collocated SSA or field maintenance unit system maintain a 30-day supply.

PRESCRIBED LOAD LIST

3-8.   Units are required to stock PLLs, which consist of demand- or nondemand-supported maintenance repair parts and initial stock repair parts for new end items. PLLs must be approved by the first general officer or equivalent staff level in the chain of command. PLLs allow units to maintain a supply of high-use, high-demand items available for quick repairs. Most PLL items are demand supported and must meet a set number of demands within a certain time period before ordering. AR 710-2 provides guidelines for maintaining PLLs.

SHOP STOCK

3-9.   Shop stocks are comprised of demand-supported repair parts and consumables stocked within a support-level maintenance activity with a support-level maintenance mission authorized by an MTOE, TDA, or joint table of allowances. These repair parts are used internally by the maintenance unit to accomplish maintenance requests or programmed repairs. AR 710-2 covers criteria for the number of demands required and items authorized to fulfill shop stocks.

AUTHORIZED STOCKAGE LIST

3-10.   The authorized stockage list (ASL) is a list of all items authorized to be stocked at specific levels to meet the logistics needs of supported aviation customers.

3-11.   The supporting SSA ASL is the supply source from which aviation units may replenish their stockage of shop stock items to authorized levels. The supporting SSA also provides a direct exchange service for repairable components.

3-12.   Demand history files are maintained to reflect the most recent 12-month period and are used to support decisions to stock items. At supply base SSAs, demand frequency files are maintained for every Class II, Class III (packaged), Class IV, and Class IX (air) item issued to aviation units. Items selected for stockage make up the ASL.

3-13.   The ASL identifies authorized items to be stocked in the SSA to support customer demands. Although an item may qualify for inclusion in the ASL, the unit item manager may or may not add it because of stockage and SSA funding constraints. The Standard Army Retail Supply System (SARSS) considers an item qualified for stockage when it is demand-supported, an operational readiness float item specifically authorized for incorporation, an initial provisioning item, and a mission-essential or mandatory stockage item.

3-14.   SARSS automatically considers ASL items receiving insufficient demand during a 180-day period for a stockage list code change or deletion from the ASL.

Authorized Stockage List Stockage Selection

3-15. Stockage selection is the decision to place an item in stock. Demand history files must be maintained to reflect the most recent 12-month period; as an automation objective, a 24-month period must be maintained and stratified to the end-item code. At the supply activity, demand frequency files must be maintained for every Class II, Class III (packaged), Class IV, and Class IX item issued to customers. Items selected for stockage make up the ASL.

3-16. Essentiality is a primary consideration in determining the range of items included in the ASL. The FEDLOG contains the essentiality code for each NSN. Repair parts selected for stockage are restricted to the following ECs: C, D, E, and J. Where a quick supply store is established, E, C, and G items are authorized for stockage. ECs are listed in DA Pam 708-2.

ADMINISTRATION

STANDING OPERATING PROCEDURES

3-17. Class II, Class III, Class VII, Class VIII, Class IX, and Class X repair parts SOPs must be written and updated to incorporate latest changes. PLL/ASL sections are usually under one supply system, and SOPs must reflect the system the command uses. Procedures specified in SOPs must conform to all applicable guidance in governing regulations, directives, and policies. SOPs should be used as a day-to-day management tool by all personnel affiliated with maintenance operations. AR 710-2 is helpful when writing supply SOPs.

IDENTIFICATION LIST

3-18. Identification lists (ILs) include narrative and illustrative descriptions of stocked items. ILs may be found by locating an item's federal supply classification (FSC) in SB 708-21 or SB 708-22 (the FSC is the first four digits of the item's NSN). All ILs are listed in numerical order by FSC in DA Pam 25-30.

FEDERAL LOGISTICS INFORMATION

3-19. Cataloging for all services has been consolidated under the Defense Logistics Integration Service, which is responsible for FEDLOG. FEDLOG is comprised of four CDs that include supplier names, addresses, and telephone numbers, as well as manufacturers, part numbers, NSNs, and ordering and pricing information for more than 12 million supply items. Data from the monthly FEDLOG are used to process and edit requests, update stock records, receive inventory, ship supplies, and process reconciliation. To subscribe to FEDLOG, ALSS personnel should send the following information to the address below:

- AMDF account number (a six-digit number beginning with zero, found on the upper-right corner of the AMDF mailing label), or request an account be established.
- Complete military mailing address.
- Make, model, and serial number of the computer and CD drive for each copy requested.
- Point of contact (POC) information, including name and telephone number.

3-20. Subscription requests should be mailed to: Commander, U.S. Army Materiel Command LOGSA, AMXLS-MLA, Bldg. 3623, Redstone Arsenal, AL 35898-7466.

LOGISTICS AND ACQUISITION OF AVIATION ORGANIZATIONAL CLOTHING AND INDIVIDUAL EQUIPMENT

3-21. The Defense Supply Center Philadelphia (DSCP) is an inventory control point within the Defense Logistics Agency. The DSCP provides food, clothing, textiles, medicines, medical equipment, and general and industrial supplies and services to America's warfighters, their eligible family members, and other non-DOD customers worldwide.

3-22. DSCP's role is to support logistics and acquisition of aviation organizational clothing and individual equipment (OCIE). The DSCP website, www.dscp.dla.mil/, contains valuable information for ALSOs, logistics officers (S4s), and CIF managers. The "customer links" section contains search tools used to locate OCIE flight items by entering an NSN or item description (nomenclature). The following information may be obtained through the site's search tools:

- NSNs.
- Sizes.
- Acquisition advice codes.
- DSCP item manager POCs.

3-23. Questions, comments, and suggestions regarding this issue may be directed via e-mail to forscompoc@forscom.army.mil.

DOCUMENTATION

3-24. Requests for equipment must be documented on DA Form 2064, which should then be maintained as a record of request. Supply personnel can provide document numbers, due-in status, and supply status. Turn-ins from the ALSS shop must be documented on DA Form 2064 when completed at the unit level or DA Form 3161 when completed by the PBO. Personnel must retain a file copy when using supply forms.

DOCUMENT REGISTER

3-25. DA Form 2064 is used to record supply transactions. Quantities requested, received, adjusted, turned in, or due in are entered on one of three types of document registers: nonexpendable, durable, and expendable. Only units authorized to submit supply requests to a direct support unit (DSU) may use the expendable register. The PBO designates by memorandum those elements within a unit authorized to request expendable supplies. Memorandums must specify the supply class, DOD activity address code, and document serial numbers the element will use. DA Pam 710-2-1 contains policies and procedures for maintaining document registers.

AUTHORIZATION TO REQUEST AND SIGN FOR SUPPLIES

3-26. Office management files must include a copy of assumption of command orders or appointing memorandums. A minimum of three copies must be sent to each DSU from which supplies are drawn, along with an accompanying DA Form 1687 (Notice of Delegation of Authority-Receipt for Supplies) for requesting and signing for supplies. The office must retain one copy and send two copies to the DSU (one copy each for the editing and issuing/receiving sections). If possible, different people should be designated to perform these actions. DA Pam 710-2-1 and AR 725-50 outline procedures to reduce potential fraud, waste, and abuse.

REQUISITION

3-27. Local procedures regarding how unit personnel request equipment and repair parts from supply sections differ throughout the Army. Commanders may require requests to be made on memorandums or official supply forms. Regardless of these procedures, ALSS personnel must be able to provide the following information to supply personnel:

- NSNs.
- Part numbers.
- Nomenclatures.
- Supply sources.
- Acquisition advice codes.
- Materiel category structure codes.
- Sources of information (Army logistics, FEDLOG, or medical category).
- Publications, pages, paragraphs, figures, and/or item numbers.
- Units of issue.
- Quantities.
- DOD identification codes and Class V items.

PRIORITY

3-28. The uniform materiel movement and issue priority system must be determined before repair parts are requested. The unit's force activity designator (found in the unit's permanent activating orders) and urgency of need designator (UND) determine request importance. Commanders are responsible for assigning priority designators; they or a delegated representative must review all requests with UNDs of A or B. UND tables are provided in DA Pam 710-2-1.

SCREENING AUTHORITY

3-29. The unit commander must designate in writing which section personnel have authority to screen repair part requests. The individual authorized to process requests should first check each request for correct priority designators. He or she also must initial DA Form 2064 and DA Form 2765 or 2765-1 and approve all high priority (01 through 08) requests.

SUPPLY STATUS

3-30. Supply status informs requesters of the supplier's decision on a specific supply request and is provided by the DSU via status cards, listings, or diskettes. Supply status is noted using status codes found in DA Pam 710-2-1.

3-31. A due-in status file for each document register must be kept on file in the ALSE shop. Cards must be filed in document number sequence when status is received for open-part requests.

SUPPLY MANAGEMENT

3-32. All available diagnostics equipment should be used to determine the causes of malfunctions before parts are replaced. The accomplishment of training and mission objectives within available resources depends upon reducing dollars spent on repairable part replacement. This reduction requires that unserviceable and economically repairable parts be repaired at the lowest level possible, if not precluded by policy or capability. Fault repair requires a mechanic or technician to perform an initial, accurate diagnosis of all equipment, component, assembly, and subassembly malfunctions; order repair parts; and make repairs immediately. This process ensures users do not waste manpower resources troubleshooting failures and replacing components needlessly.

EQUIPMENT, COMPONENT, SUPPLIES, AND MATERIEL STORAGE

3-33. ALSE, support equipment, components, supplies, and other materiel must be stored according to the item's appropriate technical publication per AR 95-1, AR 190-11, AR 710-2, DA Pam 385-64, and DA Pam 710-2-1. Pyrotechnic storage and inventory must follow guidance in ammunition and explosive standards and local policies. Flammables must be stored according to existing DOD, command, and local policies and regulations. All cabinets, bins, and storage facilities must be marked to identify equipment, components, supplies, and materiel stored within them. In addition, ALSS maintenance program managers must ensure, initiate, and maintain appropriate updated inventory documentation.

3-34. Suitable storage racks, cabinets, and shelves should be fabricated or purchased to accommodate specific equipment. Storage shelves should be free from rough or abrasive materials and splinters. Wood or metal shelves may be covered with rubber matting or tile. Hangers should be constructed of wood or heavy plastic material. Equipment storage areas must be well ventilated, out of direct sunlight, and adequately lit. To reduce mildew and corrosion, storage areas should be climatically controlled from 60 °F to 75 °F at less than 60 percent relative humidity. Lockable storage cabinets must be provided to secure ALSE and support equipment.

SECTION III – AUTOMATED SUPPLY MANAGEMENT

UNIT LEVEL LOGISTICS SYSTEM

3-35. There are three versions of the Unit Level Logistics System (ULLS): ULLS-Ground (ULLS-G), ULLS-Aviation (ULLS-A), and ULLS-Supply (ULLS-S4). Each system performs slightly different functions. Additional information on ULLS may be found in ATTP 3-04.7 (FM 3-04.500).

STANDARD ARMY MAINTENANCE SYSTEM

3-36. The Standard Army Maintenance System (SAMS) provides commanders and maintenance managers with accurate and timely maintenance management and logistics information from the Army Sustainment Command. SAMS provides information on inoperable equipment and required repair parts, as well as selected maintenance and equipment readiness and performance reports. It also provides LOGSA with work order data for equipment performance and other analyses. SAMS is comprised of SAMS-Level 1 (SAMS-1) and SAMS-Level 2 (SAMS-2). When fielded, SAMS-Enhanced (SAMS-E) will replace SAMS-1, SAMS-2, and ULLS-G. Additional information on SAMS may be found in ATTP 3-04.7 (FM 3-04.500).

STANDARD ARMY RETAIL SUPPLY SYSTEM

3-37. SARSS is a multiechelon supply management and stock control system. SARSS is comprised of SARSS-Level 1 (SARSS-1) at the direct support level; SARSS-Level 2A/C (SARSS-2A/C) or corps/theater automated data processing service center; and SARSS-Gateway. SARSS provides supply data to the integrated logistics analysis program system at various functional levels. Additional information on SARSS may be found in ATTP 3-04.7 (FM 3-04.500).

GLOBAL COMBAT SUPPORT SYSTEM-ARMY

3-38. The Army is transitioning its logistics processes from an echeloned, mass inventory approach to a more efficient and responsive distribution system based on the availability and use of accurate information. As part of this process transformation, the Army is moving away from multiple, stand-alone custom software applications to an integrated, commercial enterprise resource planning solution. The Army will connect the national and tactical logistics domains through a program called Global Combat Support System-Army (GCSS-Army). GCSS-Army consists of two components, field/tactical and product lifecycle management plus.

SECTION IV – LOGISTICS SUPPORT ACTIVITY

LOGISTICS INTEGRATED DATABASE

3-39. LOGSA is leveraging technology to provide immediate access to its many web-based tools, including the logistics integrated database (LIDB), parts tracker, and other capabilities. LOGSA logistics products and services include sustainment tools in support of equipment readiness for users, maintainers, and managers of the Army's aircraft systems, subsystems, and weapons systems. These logistics tools contribute both independently and collectively to the Army's transformation goals by reducing the logistics footprint.

3-40. The LIDB stores national and tactical historical information and provides real-time status of Army readiness, requisition, supply, and maintenance and asset information to customers worldwide. The information needed to equip, arm, move, and sustain warfighters and fix and fuel their equipment and corresponding systems may be accessed from one central source, using one logon identification and password. LIDB system access request forms are available online at www.logsa.redstone.army.mil.

Chapter 4

Aviation Life Support Equipment Shop

CONTENTS

4-1. ALSS shop design and square footage is based on unit size and equipment density and type. Shop layout should provide protection from pilferage, dampness, fire, dust, insects, rodents, and direct sunlight. Layout also should restrict access to ALSS personnel only. Shops without internally plumbed oxygen may have floors constructed of organic or inorganic materials such as concrete that can be painted or covered with tile. To reduce the amount of combustible materials, shops with internally plumbed oxygen should have floors constructed of unpainted inorganic materials such as concrete or ceramic tile. These measures reduce the possibility of fire should an oxygen leak occur. Additional information may be found in chapter 11, TM 1-1500-204-23-1.

4-2. Commanders must evaluate building space and select an area that supports their ALSS shop maintenance program. Selection is a critical factor that allows ALSETs suitable space to perform their daily duties, which include equipment inspection and maintenance. In addition, potential shop sites should provide adequate space for—

- Use and storage of support equipment.
- Storage of repair parts and components.
- Storage of medical supplies.
- Storage of expendable and consumable materials (including hazardous material [HAZMAT]).

4-3. Shop layout should incorporate areas for a computer, printer, and hardware. Computers should have access to Internet connections.

LOCATION

4-4. ALSS shops should be located in an area removed from excessive vibration, noise, and dust. Entrances should be limited and preferably have a controlled-entry Dutch door or controlled-entry counter for equipment issue and initial inspection.

WORK AREA

4-5. Workbenches must be free of rough or abrasive materials and splinters. Bench tops should be constructed of nonporous material resistant to chipping and peeling. Benches should contain drawers for storing tools and small parts. Work areas should be well lit and contain easily accessible electrical outlets. Benches in oxygen-equipped ALSS shops should be outfitted with individual explosion-proof lighting. Additional ALSS shop and work area criteria may be found in TM 1-1500-204-23-1. A sample work area is depicted in figure 4-1 (page 4-2).

4-6. Work areas should be accessible to hot and cold running water for equipment cleaning. A stainless steel basin should be installed in oxygen-equipped ALSS shops for cleaning breathing equipment.

Figure 4-1. Sample work area

STORAGE AREA

4-7. Storage racks, cabinets, and shelves should be fabricated to accommodate specific equipment. Storage shelves should be free of rough or abrasive materials and splinters. Wood or metal shelves may be covered with rubber matting or tile. Hangers should be constructed of wood or heavy plastic material. Storage areas should be well ventilated, out of direct sunlight, and well lit. Lockable storage cabinets should be provided to secure test equipment, tools, other equipment, and supplies. A sample storage area is depicted in figure 4-2.

Figure 4-2. Sample storage area

FITTING AREA

4-8.   Fitting areas must be well lit and allow adequate space for personnel to be fitted with equipment such as vests, helmets, and harnesses. A 60-square-foot (4-foot by 15-foot) area allows space for fitting one person at a time. The fitting area should be located in the work area, as depicted in figure 4-3.

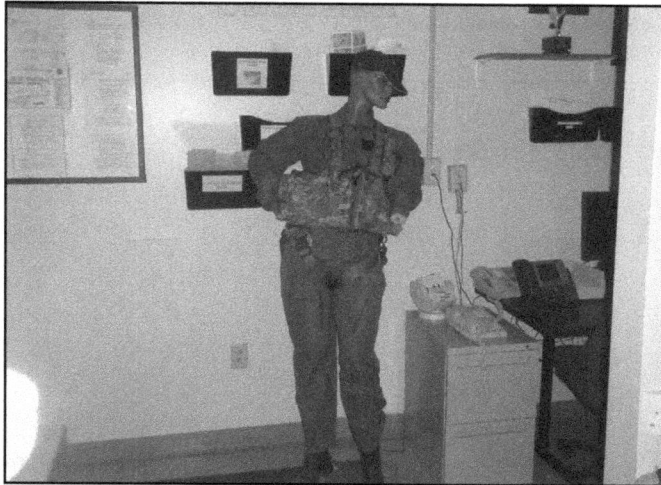

Figure 4-3. Sample fitting area

OFFICE SPACE

4-9.   A desk and other administrative equipment and supplies should be located near the shop entrance. Charts, status boards, graphs, records, and administrative supplies should be placed within reach of the desk for ease of maintenance management and record keeping, as depicted in figure 4-4.

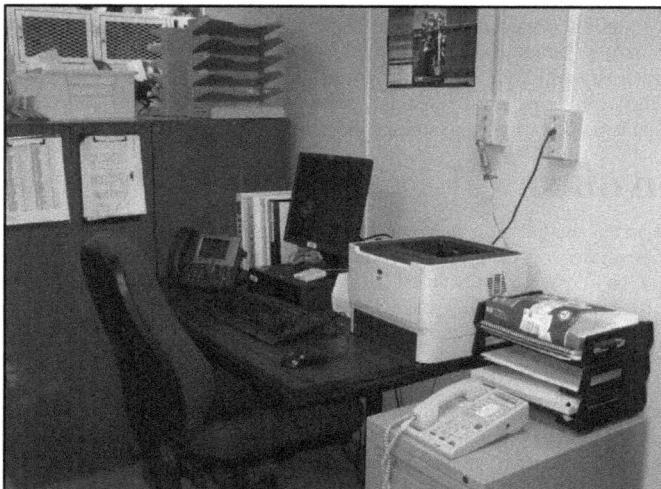

Figure 4-4. Sample office space

SUPPORT EQUIPMENT

4-10. Support equipment required to maintain ALSE varies throughout the Army due to differing geographical areas and mission requirements. Basic equipment such as hand tools, test sets, refrigerators, vacuum sealers, sewing machines, and microwaves are common among all units. It should be noted, however, that there are no standard or authorized ALSE tool kits currently in the Army inventory. Specialized equipment used to maintain flotation and oxygen equipment is specified in appropriate TMs. Equipment manuals also list common tools required to perform maintenance in MACs. A sample of commonly used support equipment is depicted in figure 4-5.

Figure 4-5. Sample support equipment

ENVIRONMENTAL CONTROL

4-11. Adequate heating and air conditioning systems are required in ALSS shops to prevent damage to equipment and supplies (especially medical supplies) from mildew, hot and cold extremes, and contamination from dust, dirt, and other foreign material. Temperature should range between 60 °F and 75 °F at 60 percent relative humidity and with the provision of filtered air. ALSS shop establishment is critical during deployments; all shops must meet the requirements noted above, if possible, depending upon location and available work shelters and storage areas.

PERSONAL HYGIENE

4-12. ALSS personnel should present a neat and clean appearance at all times. Smoking, eating, and drinking are not permitted on or around workbenches. Personnel with skin diseases or contagious viral infections must not be allowed to work in ALSS shops. Unit safety personnel and a representative from the flight surgeon's office must periodically inspect shops in accordance with regulations and unit SOP.

SHOP SAFETY

4-13. Safety practices and procedures must be followed in accordance with AR 385-10 and unit SOP. Specific safety precautions pertaining to flotation, survival, and medical and oxygen equipment are discussed in each specific item's reference publications.

Chapter 5

Aviation Life Support System and Survival Training Programs

The Army continually trains to develop and maintain combat-ready Soldiers, leaders, and units that can perform assigned tasks to specific standards. Training requirements continue even during wartime and especially within combat zones. Training builds self-confidence, promotes teamwork and esprit de corps, and increases professionalism in Soldiers, leaders, and units. This chapter establishes basic doctrine for unit/crew member survival and ALSS training requirements within aviation units. Based upon mission requirements, the ALSS training program establishes the framework for aviation units and crew members to effectively function, sustain combat capability, and survive.

OVERVIEW

5-1. ALSS and survival training must be conducted according to AR 95-1, AR 350-30, AR 350-50, and this TC. The following additional reference materials and websites should be considered when planning, developing, and administering ALSS and survival training programs:

- Air Force Regulation 64-4.
- FM 3-05.70.
- Graphic Training Aid 21-7-1.
- TC 21-3.
- TC 21-21.
- TC 1-210.
- FM 5-19.
- Joint Services Air Land Sea Applications Center:
  http://www.alsa mil.
- U.S. Army Institute For Professional Development–Correspondence:
  http://www.atsc.army mil/accp/aipdnew.asp.
- U.S. Air Force Rescue Coordination Center:
  http://www.1af.acc.af mil/units/afrcc/.
- Defense Prisoner of War/Missing Personnel Office:
  http://www.dtic.mil/dpmo/.
- Defense Supply Center–Maps Facility:
  http://www.dscr.dla.mil/rmf/products/aero/aero htm.
- Joint Services Electronic Library:
  http://www.dtic.mil/doctrine/.
- U.S. Navy Survival, Evasion, Resistance, and Escape School:
  https://www netc navy mil/centers/csf/.
- Defense Visual Information:
  http://www.defenseimagery.mil/index.html.

5-2. Additional electronic media and training materials may be requested through PM-AW's extranet website or by contacting the PM-AW logistics section via e-mail at aw-web@peoavn.redstone.army.mil. Requests may also be sent via standard mail to: Interactive Multimedia Instruction, Army AMCOM, SFAE-AV-AES-L, Redstone Arsenal, AL 35898-5000.

RESPONSIBILITIES

5-3. ALSS and survival training programs are planned, developed, administered, and documented by school-qualified ALSOs with assistance from ALSNCOs or ALSETs. All new crew members must receive an equipment briefing and orientation during their initial ALSE inspection and fitting.

AVIATION LIFE SUPPORT SYSTEM TRAINING PROGRAM

5-4. The ALSS training program must be conducted annually and include the following subject areas:
- Aircrew body armor.
- Flight helmets.
- Flight clothing.
- Aviation survival kits and components.
- First aid kits.
- Survival vests and components.
- Aircrew restraint harnesses.
- Survival transmitters and receivers.

5-5. The following areas should be trained annually to personnel assigned to units with specific missions related to or operating in specific areas or environments:
- Carried and worn subcomponents.
- Antiexposure suits.
- Oxygen systems.
- Flotation equipment.
- Overwater equipment.
- Protective equipment.
- Survival training.

5-6. In addition, ALSOs must ensure all crewmembers are trained annually in the following subject areas:
- Operator care and use of flight helmets, survival vests, survival radios, protective flight clothing, aircraft survival kits, first aid kits, emergency locator beacons, and aircrew CBRN protective equipment.
- Unit CIF procedures (issue, direct exchange, and turn in).
- Aircraft emergency egress devices and methods.

OVERWATER SURVIVAL TRAINING

5-7. Overwater survival is an integral part of aviation operations for crew members required to perform missions beyond the glide distance of land. Overwater survival training is comprised of three components: shallow water egress trainer (SWET), modular egress training simulator (METS), and emergency breathing system (EBS). Helicopter crews performing overwater operations requiring flotation devices or deck landing operations should be SWET or METS qualified and current and carry an approved EBS. These crew members must also meet currency requirements in accordance with AR 95-1 or appropriate regulations. Overwater survival training should be incorporated in the initial flight training syllabus. Unit S3s may coordinate this training through POCs found at the following websites:
- www.nomi.med.navy.mil.
- https://www.netc.navy.mil/.

DESTRUCTION OF EQUIPMENT TO PREVENT ENEMY USE

5-8. The following paragraphs provide information regarding destruction of ALSE to prevent enemy use. It is intended to be an aid to commanders, aviators, crew members, ALSOs, ALSNCOs, ALSETs, and staff members planning and conducting such training, which should focus TTP on the task of ALSE destruction.

ENEMY USE OF CAPTURED AVIATION LIFE SUPPORT EQUIPMENT

5-9. The decision for downed crews to destroy ALSE is a "final event driven action" made if capture by enemy forces is imminent.

5-10. ALSE is vital to a down crew member's survival, evasion, and safe recovery, as well as maintaining radio communications with rescue forces and other crew members. Captured ALSE might be used by enemy forces to deceive and ambush rescue aircraft or other evaders. ALSE also might provide enemy intelligence officers with information regarding the crew's origin and unit's survival equipment ensemble.

SECURITY CLASSIFICATION STATEMENT

5-11. Survival, Evasion, Resistance, and Escape (SERE) C training includes the disclosure of some classified information. Instructors must provide a briefing on the disposition and safeguarding of this information. SERE C instruction is limited to DOD and U.S. joint services military personnel only.

AUTHORITY TO DESTROY EQUIPMENT

5-12. Crews must be briefed on specific instructions for destroying downed aircraft and equipment before conducting missions in hostile or combat areas.

5-13. Per JP 3-50.21, theater special instructions (SPINS) must contain provisions for destruction of downed equipment. The S2/S3 section is responsible for conducting SPINS briefings before combat missions. Units must incorporate these procedures in their tactical SOPs.

5-14. Theater commanders have authority to destroy aircraft to prevent enemy capture. Downed crews are responsible for making the equally sensitive decision to destroy ALSE.

PROCEDURES FOR DESTROYING AVIATION LIFE SUPPORT EQUIPMENT

5-15. TM 750-244-1-2 contains procedures for destroying ALSE. If ALSE cannot be evacuated to safe areas or capture by enemy forces is imminent, it should be destroyed beyond repair and use.

5-16. Time constraints may prohibit an easy or safe destruction method. The most common technique is destruction by fire, with destruction by explosives second.

5-17. If engineer equipment is available at base camps under enemy attack or control, ALSE may be buried deep in the ground. Deep lakes, rivers, and ponds also may used to safely hide ALSE.

This page intentionally left blank.

Appendix A

Aviation Life Support System Maintenance Management and Training Standing Operating Procedures

This appendix is designed as a reference to assist units in developing SOPs related to ALSS maintenance management and training programs. Table A-1 provides a sample ALSS SOP.

Table A-1. Sample Aviation Life Support System standing operating procedure

1. SUBJECT. The subject of this SOP is (unit name) ALSE system maintenance management and training programs.

2. GOAL. The goal is to inform all Soldiers in the (unit name) of compliance requirements with ALSE regulations and policies.

3. STANDARDS

    a. References. ALSS maintenance management and training programs within the (unit name) will comply with the following references:

- AR 25-400-2, AR 95-1, AR 190-11, AR 190-13, AR 190- 51, AR 385-64, AR 385-95, AR 600-106, AR 702-6, and AR 710-2.
- CTA 50-900.
- DA Pam 25-30, DA Pam 385-40, DA Pam 385-64, DA Pam 385-95, DA Pam 710-2-1, DA Pam 710-2-2, DA Pam 738-750, and DA Pam 738-751.
- ATTP 3-04.7 (FM 3-04.500).
- TC 3-04.72 (FM 3-04.508).
- SB 742-1.
- TB 9-1300-385.
- TM 1-1500-204-23-1, TM 5-4220-202-14, TM 43-0001-37, TM 55-1680-317-23&P, and TM 55-1680-322-12.

    b. Additional guidance. Other higher headquarters' guidance includes the following:

- ALSS advisory messages.
- ARMS commander's guide.
- Additional references are in the bibliography.

4. PURPOSE. The purpose of this SOP is to establish responsibilities, policies, and general procedures applicable to the ALSS program and ensure maximum reliability and safety from all ALSE used by crew members assigned to (unit name).This SOP describes the ALSS maintenance management and training programs for all crew members engaging in aerial flights in accordance with AR 95-1, TC 3-04.72 (FM 3-04.508), and all other applicable TMs and operator's manuals. It also provides additional local (unit name) operational procedures in accordance with AR 95-1, TC 3-04.72 (FM 3-04.508), and all other applicable TMs and operator's manuals regarding storage, inspection, maintenance, cleaning, repair, and replacement of ALSE.

5. SCOPE. All personnel participating in aerial flight as crew members, non-crew members, or passengers using aircraft assigned to the (unit name) will adhere to the requirements established in this SOP. Applicable portions of Army, Air Force, and Navy TMs, TOs, and regulations will be used to devise policies, procedures, and directives for crew members and aviation life support personnel.

6. MISSION. The unit commander's mission for ALSS maintenance management and training programs is to provide safe, operationally ready ALSE and training to crew members and passengers and to inspect, maintain, and repair ALSE assigned to the (unit name).

Table A-1. Sample Aviation Life Support System standing operating procedure

7. OBJECTIVES. ALSS maintenance management and training program objectives are to—
• Provide support for all crew members assigned to (unit name).
• Ensure all crew members are properly equipped to perform their missions.
• Provide training in the care and use of all assigned ALSE.
8. DEFINITIONS
   a. ALSS: ALSS consists of components, techniques, and training required to ensure crews have the best possible flight environment. ALSS provides maximum functional capabilities of flight personnel throughout all environments experienced during normal missions. ALSS also affords the means to enhance safe and reliable escape, survival, and recovery in combat and emergency situations. Additionally, ALSS operators and training equipment provide units the ability to train and sustain crew member proficiency in the use of ALSE and supporting ALSS equipment.
   b. ALSE: ALSE comforts, sustains, and protects crew members throughout the flight environment. ALSE also provides crew members with additional protection from impact and postcrash fire. It enhances the means to escape, evade, and survive for recovery in combat or any hostile environment.
9. RESPONSIBILITIES
   a. Commander. The commander establishes the importance and tailors the functions of the ALSS section to support the unit's mission. He or she provides the logistical support and manpower to enable the ALSS shop to operate according to both its mission and applicable regulations. The commander—
• Implements ALSS policies and procedures.
• Ensures proper training, budgeting, and availability of ALSE.
• Provides trained personnel for ALSE maintenance and inspection.
• Monitors the ALSS program by—
    ■ Conducting quarterly visits at the ALSS shop.
    ■ Reviewing results from semiannual safety surveys.
    ■ Reviewing results from formal FORSCOM ARMS and Directorate of Evaluation and Standardization inspections.
    ■ Discussing ALSS issues during quarterly safety council/ALSS steering council meetings.
• Integrates ALSS into the unit's operations.
• Assigns qualified ALSS personnel and assets according to AR 95-1 to accomplish the ALSS and SERE training programs.
• Ensures the program is enforced, including separate unit participation.
   b. Flight surgeon. The unit flight surgeon is responsible for training both the physiological aspects of flight and medical considerations in survival situations. The flight surgeon will monitor the fitting and use of ALSE by crew members. He or she also will—
• Conduct physiological training for aircrew personnel.
• Monitor medical aspects of survival training for aircrew personnel.
   c. Theater, corps, and regimental, divisional, and battalion level ASO. The ASO will monitor all aviation activities for the commander to ensure proper use of protective clothing and ALSE. The ASO periodically will conduct ARMS checks on the ALSS shop.
   d. Regimental ALSO. If applicable, the regimental ALSO will—
• Review this SOP annually (at a minimum) and implement changes to comply with applicable regulations and procedures.
• Periodically inspect battalion ALSS shops using the ARMS guide.
   e. Battalion ALSO (BNALSO). The BNALSO—
• Is appointed on orders to assist, advise, and represent the battalion commander in all matters pertaining to the ALSS.
• Reviews, analyzes, and develops procedures to ensure the planning, budgeting, and maintenance of ALSS.
• Conducts a quarterly review of the ALSS shop using the aviation resources management survey commander's guide and documents results in the ALSS quarterly file.
• Ensures training of aircrew personnel in survival techniques and the proper use and maintenance of survival equipment.
• Supervises the ALSS section and ensures qualified personnel are available for conducting life support and survival training and ALSE maintenance.

Table A-1. Sample Aviation Life Support System standing operating procedure

- Keeps a current file of regulations, procedures, and TMs pertaining to inspection, maintenance, and use of ALSE.
- Ensures units encourage life support suggestions and operational hazard reports.
- Ensures materiel deficiency reports are submitted for ALSE that fails to operate as designed.
- Participates as a member of the unit aviation safety council.
- Assists higher headquarters in standardizing the ALSS program.

f. Battalion ALSNCO. The ALSNCO—
- Is appointed on orders to assist, advise, and represent the BNALSO or company ALSO in all matters pertaining to ALSE.
- Establishes a library of regulations, procedures, and TMs pertaining to inspection, maintenance, accountability, and stockpile reliability (surveillance) and use of assigned ALSE.
- Reviews and updates the ALSS library quarterly.
- Maintains files and a status board recording ALSE inspection due dates.
- Ensures flight operations and line company ALSOs receive monthly updates of crewmember ALSE inspection status and inspection due dates.
- Ensures all ALSE is maintained in a high state of mission readiness through inspecting, cleaning, fitting, testing, and repair.
- Participates in local ALSS steering council meetings.
- Inspects all controlled drugs, if used, according to AR 40-61.
- Participates as an enlisted ALSS representative at aviation safety meetings.
- Establishes shop stock and maintains current inventory records.

g. Company/Facility ALSO. The company/facility ALSO—
(1) Will be school trained and appointed on orders to assist and represent the commander in all matters pertaining to the ALSS shop.
(2) The company/facility ALSO is responsible for—
- Reviewing, analyzing, and developing procedures for planning, budgeting, and maintaining an ALSS maintenance management and training program.
- Ensuring crew members are trained in survival techniques and the proper operation, use, and maintenance of survival equipment.
- Supervising the life support section and ensuring qualified personnel are available for organizational-level ALSS maintenance and survival training.
- Keeping a current file of regulations and procedures and maintaining a library of TMs pertaining to the maintenance, accountability and stockpile reliability (surveillance), care, use, and training of assigned life support and survival equipment.
- Ensuring unit personnel have adequate information and training before using new equipment or system changes.
- Ensuring unit personnel encourage life support suggestions and operational hazard reports.
- Ensuring materiel deficiency reports are submitted on life support equipment failing to operate as designed.
- Participating as a member of the unit's aviation safety council representing ALSS.
- Assisting higher headquarters in standardizing ALSS maintenance management and training programs.

h. ALSETs. ALSETs will—
- Be school trained and appointed on unit orders to assist, advise, and represent the ALSO in all matters pertaining to ALSS.
- Establish a library of TMs pertaining to the care, use, maintenance, accountability and stockpile reliability (surveillance), and training of assigned aviation life support and survival equipment.
- Maintain ALSE in a high state of serviceability through inspecting, cleaning, testing, fitting, adjusting, replacing, and repairing.
- Maintain files on inspection, maintenance, lot numbers, expiration dates, work orders, and supply pertaining to ALSS operations.
- Participate as a member of unit-level or higher enlisted aviation safety councils.

Table A-1. Sample Aviation Life Support System standing operating procedure

- Complete and submit parts and equipment requisitions to appropriate requisitioning offices or agencies (both within and outside the unit).
- Assist the unit ALSO or commander's designated representative with the ALSS training program.

i. Pilots-in-command (PCs). PCs will—

- Ensure ALSE appropriate for the mission and operational environment is available on the aircraft.
- Ensure crew members and passengers are briefed on ALSE location and use.
- Provide ALSS personnel as much notice as possible to prepare appropriate ALSE for all flight modes and geographical environments expected and ensure equipment is serviceable for the duration of the flight/mission.

j. Crew members. Crew members will—

- Ensure ALSE appropriate for the mission and operational environment is available on the aircraft and crew members are briefed on its location and use.
- Ensure crew member ALSE preflight checks are conducted according to appropriate operator's manuals before every flight.
- Ensure all ALSE accessible for use by crew members, including survival vests, first aid kits, overwater survival kits, and aircraft modular survival system (AMSS) kits, is serviceable for the flight and not overdue for inspection.
- Ensure all crew members participating in the flight do not fly with any ALSE overdue for inspection or found to be unserviceable during the preflight inspection.
- Maintain possession of survival equipment unless it has been turned in for repair or inspection.
- Conduct a preflight inspection of personal ALSE to ensure it is current and serviceable before flight.
- Adhere to ALSE inspection due dates and ensure equipment is turned in to the ALSS shop before its expiration.
- Use individual storage lockers provided by the command to store and secure individual ALSE.
- Ensure individual ALSE preflight checks are conducted according to appropriate operator's manuals before every flight.
- Ensure any ALSE overdue for inspection or found to be unserviceable during the preflight inspection is not used during flight.
- Immediately report lost, damaged, or destroyed ALSE to their company ALSO, company ALSNCO, or ALSS shop.

10. AIRCRAFT EQUIPMENT REQUIREMENTS. PCs will ensure all crewmembers and passengers are briefed before each flight on the location and use of life support equipment onboard the aircraft. The following ALSE is required at a minimum for all flights:

- Survival vest worn by each crew member.
- At least one survival radio.
- One survival kit per aircraft.
- Panel-mounted first aid kits: One per crew compartment and one per every five passenger seats installed or fraction thereof according to TM 1-1500-204-23-1.

11. PREFLIGHT PROCEDURES

a. Radio set, personal radio communicator (PRC)-90/PRC-90-2

- Exposed metal surfaces (casing): Inspect all metal surfaces for signs of rust or corrosion.
- Wrist straps: Inspect for mildew, fungus, dry rot, or insect damage.
- Battery cap and retainer: Check for proper installation, assembly, broken retainer, and internal corrosion.
- Battery life: Ensure battery has a 3-year service life from the manufacture date.
- Antenna: Check for corrosion, cross-threading, or bent connector parts and deterioration of rubber cover.
    Note. The antenna on the PRC-90-2 must not exceed a 20-degree bend angle when extended.
- Battery: Remove battery and check both contacts for corrosion and mercury leakage.
- Headset, electrical: Remove earphone from its case and check for signs of corrosion or insulation breakdown and clean ear piece.
- Case, headset: Check case for loose snap or material breakdown.

Table A-1. Sample Aviation Life Support System standing operating procedure

- Controls: Turn radio on and ensure audible noise can be heard on both VOICE channels (243.0 and 282.8) from the LISTEN speaker and detent action operates without binding.
- Hermetic switch seals: Check for cracks and deterioration in the high power beacon (Hi PWR BCN), modular carrier wave, and push-to-talk (PTT) switch covers.
- Replacement: If radio appears unsatisfactory, return it to the ALSS shop.

b. Radio set, PRC-112

- Antenna: Ensure antenna rotates 90 degrees from vertical.
- Front panel: Inspect for cracks, breaks, and loose or cracked earphone connectors.
- Rear panel and case: Inspect for cracks, breaks, and loose or missing screws.
- Battery connector: Inspect for worn or cracked contacts.
- Controls: Check control tightness by rotating and checking free operation and proper detent.
- PTT switch: Check PTT operation.
- Antenna: Check for cracks and breaks.
- Earphone: Check for cracks or loose connectors.
- Battery latch: Check for damage.
- Battery: Check expiration/manufacture date (battery service life is 3 years from manufacture date).
- Screws: Check for missing or loose screws.
- Replacement: If radio appears unsatisfactory, return it to the ALSS shop.

c. Survival vest

(1) Survival vest components will be inspected for proper function and serviceability. These components include—

- Vest fabric: Inspect all fabric, including pockets, for tears, seam separation, loose stitching, and snaps.
- Slide fasteners: Inspect for proper operation.
- Mirror, strobe light, and compass: Inspect to ensure these three components are attached to the vest via lanyard.

(2) All emergency flares and signals will be maintained according to applicable TMs, TBs, and SBs regarding stockpile reliability (surveillance) requirements.

d. Head gear unit (HGU)-56 helmet

- Outer shell: Check for cracks or gouges and gently flex the helmet at the ear cups to detect cracks.
- Screws, fasteners, and buckles: Adjust to fit tightly and operate easily.
- Visor: Check for cracks, scratches, or blemishes and clean with a soft cloth.
- Visor housing: Visor should slide and adjust easily; housing should sit tight against the helmet without cracks or gouges.
- Microphone assembly: Check plugs for separation and wires for cuts or frays; ensure microphone boom adjusts and stays in place and adjustment knob is tight.
- Ear cups: Check for cracks in pads and separation from cups; check free rotation of cups in retention assembly; ensure there is a complete seal around the ears (tighten chin strap if seal is broken when rotating the head 90 degrees left or right).
- Adjustable retention assembly, suspension assembly, and chin strap: Check for fraying, dry rot, excessive oil and dirt, and loose attachment points.
- Thermal plastic liner (TPL) assembly: Check foam liner for gouges, chips, or cracks and looseness within the helmet shell; ensure all four layers are present; check black liner covering for excessive oil and dirt.

e. Integrated helmet and display sight system (IHADSS) helmet

- Outer shell: Check for cracks or gouges; gently flex the helmet at the ear cups to detect cracks.
- Screws, fasteners, and buckles: Adjust to fit tightly and operate easily.
- Visor: Check for cracks, scratches, or blemishes and clean with a soft cloth.
- Visor housing: Visor should slide and adjust easily; housing should be tight against the helmet without any cracks or gouges.
- Microphone assembly: Check plugs for separation and wires for cuts or frays; ensure microphone boom adjusts and stays in place and adjustment knob is tight.

Table A-1. Sample Aviation Life Support System standing operating procedure

- Ear cups: Check for cracks in pads and separation from cups; check free rotation of cups in retention assembly; ensure there is a complete seal around the ears (tighten chin strap if seal is broken when rotating the head 90 degrees left or right).
- Adjustable retention assembly, suspension assembly, and chin strap: Check for fraying, dry rot, excessive oil and dirt, and loose attachment points.

f. Life preserver unit (LPU)-34/P low profile flotation collar

- PCs must ensure all crew members know how to wear and deploy the LPU before use.
  - *Note.* Do not pull lanyards; this will cause the LPU to inflate.
- Inspection record (located in the survival vest's inner left bottom pocket)—
  - Ensure the LPU has not exceeded its inspection due date.
  - Straps and cell coverings: Inspect for frays, tears, holes, and security of stitching.
  - Deployment handles: Check for frays and cuts and ensure pull knobs are exposed no more than a half inch to prevent snagging inside the aircraft and inadvertent deployment of the LPU.

g. Survival kits

(1) Survival kits should not be opened for preflight inspection. Survival kit components include—

- Seal: Ensure seal is intact; if not, return kit to the ALSS shop for inspection and resealing.
- Condition tag: Ensure tag is a yellow DD Form 1574 (Serviceable Tag-Materiel) and that kit is not past its inspection due date.
- Case: Inspect for wear, holes, cracks, or separating straps.

(2) The aircraft first aid kit checklist is the same as the survival kit checklist.

12. TRAINING

a. General

(1) ALSS and SERE training will be conducted according to AR 95-1, AR 350-30, and TC 1-508. A school-qualified ALSET will administer ALSS training. The ALSO/ALSNCO will document attendance at these classes with locally produced sign-in rosters. At a minimum, the ALSO/ALSNCO will ensure training on an annual basis in survival vest use and proper care and use of emergency flares and signals. Training includes the following subject areas:

- Survival radios.
- Flight helmets.
- Flotation equipment.
- Survival kits.
- Protective clothing.
- Survival training.

(2) Additional training should include—

- Operator care and use of flight helmet, survival vest, survival radio, protective flight clothing, aircraft survival kits, first aid kits, emergency locator beacons, and aircrew CBRN protective equipment.
- Unit central issuing facility procedures (issue, direct exchange, and turn in).
- Aircraft emergency egress devices and methods.

b. Individual

(1) All new crew members will receive an equipment briefing and orientation during initial ALSE inspection and fitting.

(2) Each unit ALSO will develop an ALSS and SERE training program.

(3) The unit will have full responsibility for implementing its ALSS and SERE program and adding training to its annual training calendar.

(4) Unit ALSS and SERE trainers will be responsible for maintaining all training documentation.

(5) SERE training will be conducted according to AR 95-1, AR 350-30, AR 525-90, TC 3-04.72 (FM 3-04.508), JP 3-50.2, JP 3-50.3, and JP 3-50.21.

(6) SERE B- and C-level training will be administered only by graduates of a formal SERE C school using training planning guides approved by the AR 350-30 proponent. SERE training will include the following subject areas:

- SERE A: Code of conduct.
- SERE B: Basic land survival, food and water procurement, shelter building, fire craft, emergency signaling, basic land navigation, and combat search and rescue procedures.

Table A-1. Sample Aviation Life Support System standing operating procedure

- SERE C: Combat evasion, extraction and recovery, theater SPINS, special operations personnel and partisan linkups, exfiltration methods, prisoner of war resistance, escape, isolated personnel report (ISOPREP) procedures, and joint personal recovery agency procedures and publications.

(7) Prisoner-of-war resistance labs will not be conducted unless under the direction of the John F. Kennedy Special Warfare Center according to AR 350-30. Only qualified SERE C school graduates will administer prisoner-of-war resistance training.

(8) All unit crewmembers will have a DD Form 1833 (ISOPREP) according to AR 525-90, JP 3-50.2, JP 3-50.3, and JP 3-50.21. The battalion S2 and S3 are responsible for preparing and maintaining each crew member's ISPOREP.

13. SHOP OPERATIONS

a. Maintenance, inspections, repairs, and procedures

(1) ALSETs maintain and operate the ALSS shop. Non-ALSS school-trained technicians, designated on orders signed by the commander, are authorized to inspect and service first aid kits as specified by TM 1-1500-204-23-1, chapter 11. Equipment inspections will be accomplished within the interval specified and according to the appropriate Army TMs, TBs, SBs; Air Force publications; TOs; and NAVAIRs.

(2) ALSE serviceability will be identified with the appropriate materiel condition code tag—DD Form 1574 (Serviceable Tag-Materiel), 1577-2 (Unserviceable [Repairable] Tag-Materiel), or 1577 (Unserviceable [Condemned] Tag-Materiel)—according to DA Pam 738-751. All ALSE items that fail required inspections or tests will be tagged with the appropriate DD form. Those items that cannot be repaired locally will be referred to higher-level maintenance or turned in to supply for replacement.

(3) HGU-56/P maintenance procedures are as follows:

- HGU-56/P helmets will be inspected according to TM 1-8415-215-12&P every 120 days.

- After inspection is complete, an appropriate entry will be made on the helmet's DA Form 2408-22 (Helmet and Oxygen Mask/Connector Inspection Record) indicating inspection type (initial or 120 day), inspection completion date, and next inspection due date; the ALSE status board will then be updated.

- All HGU-56/P helmets will be marked with the aviator's name and next inspection due date on the right rear of the helmet.

- Helmet repairs will remain at the unit level; inspection and repair data will be recorded on DA Form 2408-22.

(4) IHADSS maintenance procedures are as follows:

- IHADSS will be inspected according to TM 9-1270-233-23&P every 120 days.

- After inspection is complete, an appropriate entry will be made on the helmet's DA Form 2408-22 indicating inspection type (initial or 120 day), inspection completion date, and next inspection due date; the ALSE status board will then be updated.

- All IHADSS helmets will be marked with the aviator's name and next inspection due date on the right rear of the helmet.

(5) AMSS maintenance procedures are as follows:

- AMSS will be inspected according to TM 1-1680-354-23&P every 360 days, plus or minus 6 days.

- After AMSS inspection is complete, an appropriate entry will be made on the aircraft's DA Form 2408-18 (Equipment Inspection List) indicating inspection completion date and next inspection due date.

- Inspection records will also be maintained in company AMSS logbooks, located in battalion ALSS shops.

(6) Aircraft first aid kit maintenance procedures are as follows:

- Aircraft first aid kits will be inspected according to TM 1-1500-204-23-1 every 12 months or before expiration of the first item due or 1 year after the previous inspection, whichever comes first.

- Aircraft will be equipped with at least one first aid kit per crew compartment and every five seats filled; condition and lot numbers of medical items within the kit will be recorded on a locally produced lot tracking form.

- Only school-trained ALSS personnel on specific orders to inspect aircraft first aid kits will complete these inspections.

- After the first aid kit inspection is complete, an appropriate entry will be made on the aircraft's DA Form 2408-18 indicating inspection completion date and next inspection due date.

(7) All SDU-5 (marker distress light) batteries will be tested using the battery test set (Army/Navy [AN]/test set [TS]-23) before use with unit ALSS.

Table A-1. Sample Aviation Life Support System standing operating procedure

(8) Survival vest maintenance procedures are as follows:

- Survival vests will be inspected before issue and every 120 days thereafter according to TM 55-1680-360-12; inspection/repair data will be recorded on DA Form 2408-25 (Mesh Net Survival Vest Inspection Record).
- Critical and easily lost items must be attached to the vest.
- After survival vest inspection is complete, an appropriate entry will be made on the vest's DA Form 2408-25 indicating inspection type (initial or 120 day), inspection completion date, and next inspection due date; the vest will then be tagged serviceable and the ALSE status board updated.
- When not in use, batteries from SDU-5 markers and PRC-90-2 or PRC-112 survival radios will be removed and properly stored.
- Survival vests will be inspected annually by supporting QASAS or trained ammunition inspectors (MOS 55B) according to SB 742-1 and TB 9-1300-385.

(9) PRC-90-2 radio maintenance procedures are as follows:

- PRC-90-2 radios will be inspected before issue and every 180 days thereafter according to TM 11-5820-1049-12 (PRC-90-2) with data recorded on DA Form 2408-24 (Survival Kit Inspection and Maintenance Record).
- These radios will be inspected every 120 days according to TM 11-5820-1049-12 (PRC-90-2) using the TS-24/B radio test set.
- Repairs other than replacing antenna or batteries will be work ordered to the next higher-level maintenance.

(10) PRC-112 radio maintenance procedures are as follows:

- These radios will be given a functional check before issue and every 120 days thereafter.
- These radios will be inspected every 12 months according to TM 11-5820-1037-13&P at the unit's aviation intermediate maintenance.
- Inspection/repair data will be recorded on DA Form 2408-23 (Survival Radio/Emergency Location Transmitter Inspection Record).
- Battery shelf life is 3 years from manufacture date.
- In the (name of installation) area, programmable frequencies will consist of a battalion internal (frequency) and B-Federal Aviation Administration (FAA) flight service station (frequency) to be written on the front of DD Form 1574.
- Individual survival codes will be programmed with 000000.
- Inspections will be accomplished according to ALSS/ALSE SOP.
- All PRC-112 radios and batteries will be properly tested and stored; battery shelf life will be limited according to FM 1-302, FM 1-508, ALSS messages, and appropriate publications.
- Batteries will be removed from radios and properly stored when not in use.

(11) LPU-10 life vest maintenance procedures are as follows:

- LPU-10 life vests will be inspected according to applicable TMs/PM-ACIS messages before issue and every 180 days thereafter.
- (Unit name) training LPU-10s will be marked "FOR TRAINING ONLY" in 1-inch letters.

(12) Life raft maintenance procedures are as follows:

- One-man life rafts will be inspected according to applicable TMs/PM-ACIS messages before issue and every 180 days thereafter.
- (Unit name) training one-man life rafts will be marked "FOR TRAINING ONLY" in 1-inch letters.

(13) LPU-34/P low-profile flotation collar maintenance procedures are as follows:

- LPU-34/P low-profile flotation collars will be inspected every 360 days according to NAVAIR 13-1-6.1-2.
- Inspection and repair information will be recorded on DA Form 2408-26 (Life Preserver Inspection Record); DA Form 2408-27 (Life Preserver Data) will be stored in the inner lower left survival vest pocket with the vest operator's manual and condition tag.
- (Unit name) training flotation equipment will be marked "FOR TRAINING ONLY" in 1-inch letters.

b. ALSS file maintenance

- All forms, records, and files used by (unit name) ALSS shops for conduct of the ALSS program will be maintained according to AR 25-400-2 and DA Pam 738-751 or as listed in appropriate TMs or other source material.

Table A-1. Sample Aviation Life Support System standing operating procedure

- (Unit name) ALSS shops will maintain the following publications, forms, and files. ALSS personnel will use the ALSS quarterly file to document the following:
  - Commander's quarterly review.
  - ASO quarterly review.
  - BNALSO quarterly review.
  - Quarterly reading file, which contains important information regarding changes to policies or procedures and must be reviewed quarterly by all ALSS personnel. The ALSS quarterly reading file will contain the most current (unit name) ALSS SOP. All ALSS personnel will read and initial the quarterly ALSS reading file before performing any maintenance on (unit name) ALSE.
  - An ALSS library containing appropriate manuals, regulations, publications, and messages will be available for use during ALSE inspections, maintenance, and repair. This library will be maintained by the battalion ALSNCO and reviewed quarterly for currency and accuracy. Reviewing Soldiers will document quarterly reviews in the ALSS quarterly file. The ALSS library will contain documents and regulations authorizing ALSE.
  - ALSS publication accounts will be established and maintained by (unit name).
  - The ALSNCO will review and update the ALSS library quarterly.

c. ALSS scheduled maintenance. If scheduled maintenance requirements are not completed within the time limits specified by TC 3-04.72 (FM 3-04.508), AR 95-1, DA Pam 738-751, and appropriate TMs, ALSE will not be used for flights in (unit name) aircraft. The ALSS tracking program is in place to prevent use of out-of-date ALSE by (unit name) aircrews.

d. ALSS tracking program

(1) Each (unit name) ALSS shop will maintain an ALSE status board in the ALSS shop. This board will be updated continuously and contain the following information:

- Aviators' names and ranks.
- Assigned company (or supporting company).
- Next IHADSS inspection due date.
- Next SRU-21P (aviator's survival vest) inspection due date.
- Next PRC-112 inspection due date (if applicable).

(2) To prevent crew members from inadvertently flying with ALSE past its inspection date, the following control measures are in effect:

- A computer printout of inspection due dates for each crew member will be supplied monthly to battalion flight operations.
- When a flight plan is filed, flight operations personnel will check to ensure the crew members listed on the flight plan are within their ALSE inspection dates. An additional ALSE "GO or NO GO" block has been added to all (unit name) flight plans and must be initialed by flight operations personnel before accepting flight plans.
  - (Unit name) personnel will perform an initial inspection of all equipment before use.
  - All unserviceable equipment will be turned in to supply for replacement.
  - Fitted ALSS gear will be used only by the person for whom it was intended.
  - Only school-trained ALSS technicians appointed on orders by commanders are authorized to perform maintenance on or fit ALSS equipment.

e. Accountability

(1) Authorized personnel: Only ALSS personnel are authorized to issue and receive ALSE. The door to the ALSE shop will remain locked when ALSETs are not present. Regular operating hours for the ALSS shop will be posted on the door.

(2) Proper distribution measures: Survival equipment available in limited quantities (such as PRC-112s and LPUs) will be issued according to highest probability of use (line pilots, PCs, and then instructor pilots and crew chiefs). Other crew members will be issued equipment as it becomes available.

(3) Inventories: The following equipment will be inventoried at periodic and random intervals, not to exceed semiannually:

- Radios.
- Tool boxes.

(4) Hand receipts: Crew members will sign a DA Form 2062 for all ALSE. This hand receipt will delineate the items included in the survival vest for which the individual crew member is responsible. DA Form 2062 will be resigned at the beginning of each inspection period, not to exceed 6 months.

Table A-1. Sample Aviation Life Support System standing operating procedure

(5) Missing or broken equipment: As specified in AR 710-2-1, DA Form 2062 is good for 6 months for all equipment issued from the shop. Any crewmember missing an ALSE item will notify the ALSO/ALSNCO immediately so item resupply or a report of survey (if necessary) may be initiated with minimum delay.

(6) Files and records: The ALSS shop will maintain all files and records pertaining to ALSE. The ALSS library will be maintained in the ALSS shop according to AR 340-2 and AR 340-18.

(7) Work orders: All ALSE that requires field maintenance or other supporting maintenance will be processed by work order using DA Form 2407 (Maintenance Request) at the appropriate maintenance site. The supporting element will be responsible for equipment during the servicing period and until it is received by an authorized battalion ALSS representative. The ALSET will retain a copy of the work order.

f. Supply

(1) General: Hand receipts for all nonexpendable and durable ALSE will be maintained in the unit supply office. Hand receipts will be updated for all ALSE that is force issued or turned in to the unit.

(2) Orders and resupply: Class II items will be ordered through company supply; Class VIII will be ordered through the warehouse; and Class IX items will be ordered through tech supply. The ALSS shop will receive a list of document numbers from the supply source that shows equipment is on order. If needed items cannot be acquired through normal supply channels, a memorandum signed by the supply officer/NCO stating such must be filed in the ALSS shop. ALSETs must remain consistently aware of potential shortages through continuous inventory of bench stock items.

(3) Storage: ALSE will be stored in a manner prescribed by the appropriate TM. The ALSS shop will maintain a bench stock of necessary repair parts. All serviceable equipment stored in the shop will be identified with the appropriate materiel condition tag. Excessive, unserviceable, and obsolete ALSE not required by the battalion mission will be turned in.

g. Pyrotechnics and batteries

(1) Pyrotechnics will be stored and handled according to AR 190-11, DA Pam 385-64, SB 742-1, and TRADOC Regulation 385-2, as well as current post policies. In addition—

- Pyrotechnics will be maintained in an appropriate container bearing required placards and a record of lot numbers. This record will include the lot numbers and quantity of stored pyrotechnics.
- Pyrotechnics will be inventoried semiannually.
- Pyrotechnics will be removed from survival kits and vests before boarding any civilian aircraft.
- Storage containers must be certified for use according to AR 190-11 and AR 190-51.
- Storage rooms and vaults must be issued a DA Form 4604-R (Security Construction Statement) and have an explosive storage limits and license according to DA Pam 385-64.
- All ALSE items will be checked according to SB 742-1 and TB 9-1300-385 standards and criteria.
- All ALSE items will be stored according to AR 190-11, AR 190-51, AR 710-2, and AR 385-64 requirements for physical security, accountability, inventory, and explosives safety.

(2) Batteries will be stored and disposed of in a safe manner according to the HAZMAT officer/NCO and SB 11-6.

h. ALSS corrosion preventive control (CPC)

(1) ALSE CPC inspections will be accomplished in association with inspections and maintenance according to the item's technical publications.

(2) When the ALSET documents an inspection or maintenance is complete, CPC will be considered accomplished during the action. A separate CPC inspection is not required or documented per PM-ACIS.

(3) The ALSET will use only approved materials, solvents, and POL specified in applicable technical publications.

(4) ALSS equipment storage and climate control will be used according to TC 3-04.72 (FM 3-04.508).

i. Personal equipment care

(1) Crew members will periodically clean their ALSE. All ALSE will be cleaned according to this SOP before turn-in for inspection.

(2) Flight vests may be cleaned by hand washing with a mild laundry detergent and hang dried. A conventional washer and dryer should not be used for cleaning survival vests due to the possibility of mesh damage.

(3) Flight helmets should be periodically wiped with a soft, nonabrasive cloth. In some cases, a bristle brush may be used for hard-to-reach areas. The TPL's black cover may be removed and washed by hand with a mild detergent and hang dried. TPL covers may not be dried in conventional dryers.

(4) A soft, nonabrasive cloth or soft bristle brush may be used to clean survival radios. Operators may only clean the radio's exterior surface. At no time may the operator disassemble the radio for cleaning or troubleshooting.

Table A-1. Sample Aviation Life Support System standing operating procedure

j. Termination of crew duties. Once crew members have been relieved of their duties, they are required to immediately return their ALSE to the ALSS shop for reissue. There is a shortage of ALSE within the unit, and personnel are encouraged to turn in equipment not being used. Platoon sergeants are encouraged to assist the ALSS program in this matter to ensure their Soldiers are equipped properly.

k. Inprocessing and outprocessing

(1) Inprocessing: All Soldiers on flight status arriving to (unit name) will inprocess through the (company/battalion) ALSS shop, located in the unit hangar. Aviators will turn in their flight helmet to the ALSS shop as soon as possible after arrival to expedite required inspection and maintenance. Individuals may inprocess or outprocess at any time during business hours.

(2) Outprocessing: Crew members will turn in their ALSE at least 5 working days before their clearing date so equipment can be inspected and tagged for turn in. If the Soldier is to fly up to the day of clearing, he or she must coordinate in advance with the ALSS shop.

(3) Turn-in for scheduled inspections: Crew members will turn in their flight gear at least 5 working days before its inspection due date. The ALSS shop will complete inspections within 2 working days.

l. Storage of crew member ALSE

(1) All crew members will use crew lockers to store their ALSE. All items will be readily available to the ALSET for inspection/repair.

(2) At a minimum, crew members are required to keep the following items in their assigned locker at all times, except when flying:

- Flight helmet and helmet bag.
- Survival vest.
- Life preserver.

m. ALSERP

(1) If ALSE is used during an actual accident or incident, the ALSS shop will submit the used equipment for inspection and analysis according to the ALSERP, AR 385-95, and DA Pam 385-40.

(2) All ALSS personnel will be familiar with the ALSERP according to AR 385-95 and DA Pam 385-40.

(3) Selected ALSS personnel will be appointed on written duty orders to participate on the state accident investigation team. If ALSS personnel are used as team members during aviation accident investigations, they will work under the supervision of the onsite commander.

(4) ALSS personnel will assist USAARL representatives with collecting ALSS/SERE equipment and documentation involved in aviation accidents. Equipment items will be collected, marked as accident exhibits, and shipped according to USAARL instructions. ALSS/SERE equipment involved in aviation accidents will be removed from service and not reissued until final written disposition of serviceability has been determined by USAARL.

(5) The investigating ALSET will inventory any ALSS/SERE equipment items collected from the accident site. Item accountability will be provided to the battalion S4. USAARL representatives will provide the battalion S4 with property receipts on items taken for laboratory investigation.

n. Flights on commercial air carriers

(1) Crew members flying on commercial airliners will follow FAA and airliner regulations and procedures. Survival vests contain a pocketknife, surgical razor, pyrotechnics, and carbon dioxide (CO_2) cylinders. Pyrotechnics will not be carried onboard commercial airline flights.

(2) The PC will check with the air carrier regarding its procedures for carrying knives and CO_2 cylinders.

o. ALSE mobility and deployment procedures

(1) ALSS shop organization for deployment and mobility operations will be conducted according to TC 3-04.72 (FM 3-04.508). ALSS equipment will be deployable by means of properly maintained equipment with applicable modifications, adjustments, additions, and upgrades. Any ALSE item not up to its full operational potential and standards must be corrected before deployment or at the deployment site.

(2) The (unit name) will maintain all ALSS shop bench stock and shop stock/PLL available:

- Upon mobilization, all ALSS parts will be transferred to each unit's field-level maintenance ALSS section for deployment stock:
    - Battalion: 30 percent.
    - Company: 70 percent.
- Each unit will have a bench stock/PLL written for its specific needs with the aid of a packing load list on file in the ALSS shop.

(3) The ALSS shop will maintain mobility according to the following procedures upon notification of deployment:

- The ALSET will report the status of all ALSS equipment and parts to the ALSS officer.

Table A-1. Sample Aviation Life Support System standing operating procedure

- Each unit will be provided with a percentage amount of ALSS stock according to the unit's prearranged bench stock/PLL.
- Each unit will be provided with ALSE inspection records for all assigned crew members, aircraft, and ALSS equipment.
- ALSS personnel are responsible for packing and shipping ALSS stock and support items.
- ALSS personnel will inventory tools, ALSS stock, and equipment upon arrival at the deployment site.
- The unit ALSS section will maintain the ALSS program according to TC 3-04.72 (FM 3-04.508), the battalion/company tactical SOP, and the following procedures during deployment:
  - Consolidate ALSS resources whenever possible.
  - Locate all ALSS-qualified individuals at the site.
  - Locate and inventory ALSS stock.
  - Set up an inspection and maintenance schedule according to the unit's mission schedule.
  - Set up ALSS operations according to TC 3-04.72 (FM 3-04.508).
  - Establish a contact with unit supply and the unit publications NCO.
  - Coordinate with the battalion S4 to secure adequate shelter, power, light, and water.
  - Requisition ALSS stock/PLL items and flight equipment to upgrade the unit's needs and tactical requirements.
  - Establish the ALSS training program, specifically the combat-survival portions, throughout the unit.
- Additional ALSS support and POCs should be acquired from better-equipped units such as Air Force or Navy aviation life support/parachute shops in or near the deployment area.
- Unit ALSS personnel must be prepared to conduct ALSE inspections, maintenance, and training with the immediate resources available.
- All ALSS tools and test equipment maintained at the (unit name) will be transferred to the battalion's maintenance element to support mobility shortages. The battalion S4 will be responsible for obtaining additional equipment needed to support ALSE maintenance during mobility. ALSS equipment classified as HAZMAT will be packaged, certified, and shipped according to TM 38-250.
- Procedures for HAZMAT shipment may be obtained by contacting any USAF traffic management office.
- ALSS HAZMAT shipments will be packaged and certified by qualified personnel listed in TM 38-250.

Appendix B

Tool List

Table B-1 contains the majority of items used for daily ALSE repair functions. This list may not include all tools and items required in a particular ALSE shop.

Table B-1. Tool list

Level	Nomenclature	NSN	Remarks/PT #/Model #
O	Sewing Machine, Med WT	3530-00-892-4629	Or similar
O	Shears, Bent Trimmer's	5110-00-203-9642	GGG-S-00278
O	Spatula, 81348	7330-00-254-4791	GGG-C-746
O	#4-40 Tap, 81348	5136-00-729-5689	GGG-T-70
O	#43 Tap Drill, 81348	5133-00-189-9289	MS15444-43
O	Square, Combination	5210-00-241-3599	GGG-S-656
O	Screwdriver Set, Jewel	5210-00-288-8739	CM3033
O	Drill, Twist, 55719	5133-00-189-9272	DBE27A
O	Drill, Twist, 19/64	5133-00-988-5706	DBC19/64
O	Drill, Electric, Portable, 40684	5133-00-935-7354	SP6039
O	Heater, Gun Type, Electric	4940-00-561-1002	8031088
O	Soldering Gun, 97049	3439-00-618-6623	D550-3
O	Multimeter, 80058	6625-01-139-2512	AN/PSM-45
O	Thermometer, Oven		Local purchase
O	Saw, Hand, Metal Cutting	5110-01-327-5171	HS5
O	Tap Handle	5120-00-277-4069	GGG-W-680
O	Screwdriver, Flat Tip	5120-00-278-1273	GGG-S-12181348
O	Oven, Baking, 01758	7310-01-364-4043	T4800
O	Ruler, Wood, 81348	7510-00-161-6217	GG-R-791
O	Respirator, Air Filter	4240-00-022-2524	GGG-M-125/6
O	Pliers, Diagonal Cut	5110-00-222-2708	GGG-P-TY1CL1
O	File Hand, 80244	5110-00-234-6551	GGG-F-325TY16CL1STA
O	Rule, Steel, Machinist's	512-00-180-9656	430C
O	Screwdriver, Flat-Tip	5120-00-278-1283	GGG-S-121-TY1CL5DEB
O	Screwdriver, Cross-Tip	5120-00-240-8716	GGG-S-121TY6CL1
O	Screwdriver, Cross-Tip	5120-012-023-7471	XST-100
O	Knife, Pocket	5110-00-240-5943	GGG-K-484
O	Punch, Center, Solid	5120-00-293-3509	GGG-P-831 TY2CLASZ5
O	Drill, Twist, 1/16, 55719	5133-00-837-7595	DBC1/16
O	Drill, Twist, 3/16	5133-00-988-5699	DBC3/16
O	Pliers, Long-Nose	5120-01-367-7254	D203-6
O	Wire Strippers	5110-01-111-6416	11045-INS
O	Knife, Craftsman's	5110-01-111-6416	GGG-K-00450
O	Awl, Scratch	5120-01-428-5131	69-007
O	Wrench, Box and Open	5120-00-228-9505	GGG-W-636
O	Rotary Cutting Tool	5130-01-014-6856	
O	Rule, Machinist's	5210-01-335-1608	GA2A
O	Drum, Sanding	5130-01-292-9860	
O	Band, Abrasive	5345-01-381-0788	
O	Screwdriver, Jeweler's	5120-01-176-3887	CM3033
O	Multimeter	6625-00-999-6282	
O	A1/ARS-6(V), AN/PRC-112	5820-01-279-5450	
O	Punch, Driver Pin	5120-00-242-3435	
O	Cutter, Nylon Webbing	5130-00-956-0081	

Table B-1. Tool list

Level	Nomenclature	NSN	Remarks/PT #/Model #
O	Needle, Sailmaker's	8315-00-163-1547	Size 14
O	Needle, Sailmaker's	8315-00-163-1531	Size 16
O	Nippers, End Cutting	5110-00-221-1499	
O	Pencil, China Marking	7520-00-223-6676	
O	Press, Hand, Chuck and Die	5120-00-880-0619	M369 and M370
O	Punch and Die, Grommet Inserting	5120-00-221-1146	
O	Razor, Surgical Preparation	6515-01-363-1212	
O	Razor, Surgical Preparation	6515-00-754-0426	
O	Sewing Machine, Med Wt	3530-01-507-4081	
O	Safety Goggles	4240-00-052-3776	
O	Face Shield	4240-00-202-9473	
O	Shears, Straight Trimmers	5110-00-161-6912	
O	Shears, Tailor's	5110-00-223-6370	
O	Punch, Leather	5110-00-596-9604	
O	Rule, Steel, Machinist's	5210-00-293-3514	
O	Awl, Saddler's	5120-00-223-8191	
O	Mallet, Rawhide	5120-00-293-3397	
O	Pliers, Cutting	5110-01-089-1240	
O	Yard Stick	5210-00-985-6610	
O	Tool, Fastener	5120-00-090-4412	
O	Chuck, Socket	5120-00-144-2084	
O	Chuck Stud	5120-00-144-2088	
O	Die, Eyelet	5120-00-144-2097	
O	Die, Button, Fastener	5120-00-343-8210	
O	Punch	5120-00-638-4265	
O	Needle, Sewing Machine	3530-00-257-2819	Size 20
O	Needle, Sewing Machine	3530-00-245-7981	Size 16
O	Sealing Iron, Electric	3540-01-386-2478	
O	Coolant Charging Kit with Adaptor	1680-01-510-1517	
O	Key, Socket Head Screw	5120-00-242-7410	
O	Cable Tie Gun N/A to McMaster-Carr		P/N:75785K39
O	Drying Tumbler, Household Laundry	3510-01-168-8511	
O	Heat Gun, General Purpose N/A to McMaster-Carr	4940-01-471-2136	P/N:3149K11
O	Cut/Melt Hot, Knife N/A to McMaster-Carr		P/N:2453A61
O	Scissors	5110-00-176-9329	
O	Sewing Machine with Zipper Foot	3530-00-892-4646	
O	Washing Machine, Household Laundry	3510-01-145-6625	
O	Syringe	6520-01-173-2081	
O	Bag, Shot, 3 lb		Local manufacture
O	Die, Cylinder, Thread Chaser	1377-01-069-4040	
O	Pump, Rotary Vacuum	4310-00-052-5015	
O	Slider and Pull Tab, #740	N/A	
O	Valve Core Tool	5120-01-354-5423	
O	Rubber/Steel Roller	5120-00-243-9401	
O	Tool Kit, Aircraft Mechanic	5180-00-323-4692	
O	Torque Wrench 0-150 inch lb	5120-00-117-3428	
O	1-3/16-inch Crows Foot		

Table B-1. Tool list

Level	Nomenclature	NSN	Remarks/PT #/Model #
O	7/8-inch Open-end Wrench		
O	Scale, Weighing	6670-00-461-9898	
O	Pail, Utility	7240-00-160-0455	
O	Vacuum Cleaner 115V-AC	7910-00-550-9115	
O	Tester, Spring Resiliency	6670-00-254-4634	
O	Gauge, Pressure	6685-00-757-1950	
O	Seat Extraction/Installation	5120-01-492-0504	109436
O	Scuba Fill Adapter	4220-01-543-5272	108325
O	O-Ring Tool, Set	5120-01-508-9981	9440-22
O	Valve Handle Tool	5120-01-398-3796	0530-35
O	Compressor Fill Adapter		1006-56
O	Valve Core Tool	5120-00-308-3809	
OF	Radio Test Set AN/PRM-32A	6625-01-013-9900	
OF	or AN/PRM-32	6625-00-803-3399	
OF	Battery Tester TS-2530/UR	6625-933-6112	
OF	TS-2530A/UR	6625-00-238-0223	
OF	Battery Test Adapter	6625-00-480-6315	V59584
OF	0.072-inch Spline Key MX-8801/PRC-90		A28715-056J (30106)
F	Voltmeter, Electronic AN/URM-145D/U	6625-01-119-7271	
F	Generator, Signal SG-1170/U	6625-01-120-3501	
F	Counter, Electronic AN/USM-459	6625-01-061-8928	
F	Multimeter AN/USM-452	6625-01-060-6804	
F	Multimeter ME-268/U	6625-00-646-9409	
F	Oscilloscope AN/USM-488	6625-01-187-7847	
F	Power Supply PP-3939/G	6130-00-985-8137	
F	6P5 Attenuator CN-1285/U	5985-00-491-4305	
F	CN-1174/U	5985-00-491-4305	
F	Tool Kit, Electronic Equipment TK-100/G	5120-00-625-0079	
F	Radio Test Set TS-24 (B)	6625-01-128-8588	
F	Antenna Wrench	5120-01-231-1012	P6-06-0024
F	Battery Terminal Adapter	5940-01-183-9113	A3-06-0920
F	Chassis Base	5975-01-183-2075	A3-06-0916
F	Tool Kit Electronic Equipment TK-101/G	5180-00-064-5178	W37483
F	Modified Inverted Cradle	6625-01-319-2829	
F	6-inch Adapter Cable	5995-01-0677	
F	Digital Voltmeter AN/USM-486	6635-01-145-2430	M23954
F	Power Supply, Regulated PP-2309C/U	6130-01-139-2541	P38314
F	I.P. Test Gauge	6658-01-334-5274	111610
F	Soft Case, I.P. Test Gauge		106362
F	Reversible Snap Ring Pliers	5120-00-283-00478	111100
F	Adjustable Spanner Wrench		107394
F	Valve Handle Tool		053035
F	Pliers, Small	5110-01-398-0313	9-45171
F	O-ring Tool, Set	5120-01-508-9981	944022
F	Magnifier with Illumination		9-BA819008
F	Strap Wrench	5120-01-461-1810	54325A22
F	Cylinder Inspection Light		9-47709
F	1/4-inch Nutdriver		9-41971

Table B-1. Tool list

Level	Nomenclature	NSN	Remarks/PT #/Model #
F	1/8-inch Hex Bit		9-AM11708
F	3/16-inch Hex Bit		9-46661
F	Medium Blade Screwdriver		9-41900
F	Crosstip Screwdriver #2		9-47436
F	3/8-inch Drive, Flex Handle		9-44363
F	3/8-inch Socket		9-43001
F	9/16-inch Socket		9-43004
F	11/16-inch Crows Foot		9-43625
F	3/4-inch Crows Foot		9-43226
F	1 3/16-inch Wrench		FC38A
F	11/16-inch Wrench		9-44388
F	7/8-inch 3/4-inch Combo Wrench		9-44584
F	5/8-inch 9/16-inch Combo Wrench		9-44592
F	3/8-inch 7/16-inch Combo Wrench		9-44572
F	1/2-inch Wrench		9-44385
F	12-inch Adjustable Wrench		9-44695
F	Work Mat		108357
F	Tool Punch		108360
F	X-ray Unit	N/A	
F	Tripod	N/A	
F	.50 Aluminum Penetrameter	N/A	
FD	Tool Kit, Electronic Equipment, TK-105/G	5180-00-610-8177	
FD	Attenuator, 20 DB, 10W	5985-01-065-9720	
FD	Antenna Connector		N/A 01-P2166OJ (94990)
FD	Battery Adapter		
FD	Program Loader	7025-01-279-5308	KY-913/PRC-112
FD	Test Set, Radio	6625-01-144-4481	AN/GRM-114A
FD	Antenna Connector Adapter		A01-P21660J (94990)
FD	Modified Earphone Adapter		A50-P21666J (94990)
FD	Radio Set, Personnel Locator, AN/ARS-6(V)5	6625-01-342-5906	
FD	Test Set, TS-4360/AYD-1	6624-01-342-3966	
FD	Facilities Test Kit	6625-01-189-7881	MK-994A/AR
FD	Attenuator, 20 DB, 10W 52 EA	5985-01-656-9720	
D	Leak Test Station		N/AMS-170 (00124)
D	Wrench, Torque	5120-00-221-7971	
D	Wrench, Torque	5120-00-943-0941	
D	Antenna Tool		AXB372 (94990)
D	0.072-inch Spline Key		28715-05
D	Resistor, Decade	6625-00-982-7811	Model DB62

Appendix C

Inspection Calendar

To use the sample inspection calendar illustrated in table C-1, locate the month the last inspection was performed, read across for the month the next inspection is due, then add or subtract. This calculation will determine the next inspection due date. If a 120-day inspection was performed on 4 January, it would be due again on 4 May with no days lost. If performed on 4 May, an inspection would be due again on 1 September (3 days lost/subtracted from 4 September). The inspection cycle for this sample is January, May, and September; however, if the inspection was completed on 1 September, it would be due again on 30 December (1 January with 2 days lost or subtracted). This calculation will automatically change the inspection cycle from January, May, and September to December, April, and August. ALSS personnel may want to perform periodic inspections early or late to spread equipment inspections throughout the three cycles or meet mission requirements; however, ALSE overdue for inspections must be properly tagged and identified.

Table C-1. Sample 90-, 120-, 180-, and 360-day inspection calendar

	Non-Leap Year (2009, 2010, 2011, 2013, etc).			
	90	120	180	360
January	Apr (-0)	May (-0)	July (-1)	Jan (-6)
February	May +1	June (-0)	Aug (-1)	Feb (-6)
March	June (-2)	July (-2)	Sep (-4)	Mar (-5)
April	July (-1)	Aug (-2)	Oct (-3)	Apr (-5)
May	Aug (-2)	Sep (-3)	Nov (-4)	May (-5)
June	Sep (-2)	Oct (-2)	Dec (-3)	June (-5)
July	Oct (-2)	Nov (-3)	Jan (-4)	July (-5)
August	Nov (-2)	Dec (-2)	Feb (-4)	Aug (-5)
September	Dec (-1)	Jan (-2)	Mar (-1)	Sep (-5)
October	Jan (-2)	Feb (-3)	Apr (-2)	Oct (-5)
November	Feb (-2)	Mar (-0)	May (-1)	Nov (-5)
December	Mar (-0)	Apr (-1)	June (-2)	Dec (-5)
	Leap Year (2012, 2016, 2020, 2024, etc).			
	90	120	180	360
January	Apr (-1)	May (-1)	July (-2)	Jan (-5)
February	May (-0)	June (-1)	Aug (-2)	Feb (-5)
March	June (-2)	July (-2)	Sep (-4)	Mar (-5)
April	July (-1)	Aug (-2)	Oct (-3)	Apr (-5)
May	Aug (-2)	Sep (-3)	Nov (-4)	May (-5)
June	Sep (-2)	Oct (-2)	Dec (-3)	June (-5)
July	Oct (-2)	Nov (-3)	Jan (-4)	July (-5)
August	Nov (-2)	Dec (-2)	Feb (-4)	Aug (-5)
September	Dec (-1)	Jan (-2)	Mar (-1)	Sep (-5)
October	Jan (-2)	Feb (-3)	Apr (-2)	Oct (-5)
November	Feb (-2)	Mar (-0)	May (-1)	Nov (-5)
December	Mar (-0)	Apr (-1)	June (-2)	Dec (-5)

This page intentionally left blank.

Glossary

SECTION I – ACRONYMS AND ABBREVIATIONS

ACIS	Aircrew Integrated Systems
ALSE	aviation life support equipment
ALSERP	Aviation Life Support Equipment Retrieval Program
ALSET	aviation life support equipment technician
ALSMS	Automated Life Support Management System
ALSNCO	aviation life support equipment noncomissioned officer
ALSO	aviation life support equipment officer
ALSS	Aviation Life Support System
AMCOM	U.S. Army Aviation and Missile Command
AMDF	Army Master Data File
AMPS	aviation mission planning system
AMSS	aircraft modular survival system
AN	Army/Navy
AR	Army regulation
ARMS	aviation resource management survey
ASI	additional skill identifier
ASL	authorized stockage list
ASO	aviation safety officer
ATTP	Army tactics, techniques, and procedures
AW	Air Warrior
BNALSO	battalion aviation life support equipment officer
CAGE	commercial and Government entity
CBRN	chemical, biological, radiological, and nuclear
CIF	central issue facility
CO₂	carbon dioxide
CPC	corrosion preventive control
CTA	common table of allowances
DA	Department of the Army
DA Pam	Department of the Army pamphlet
DD	Department of Defense (form)
DOD	Department of Defense
DSCP	Defense Supply Center Philadelphia
DSN	defense switch network
DSU	direct support unit
EBS	emergency breathing system
EDM	electronic data management
EIR	equipment improvement recommendation
ETM	electronic technical manual

F	Fahrenheit
FAA	Federal Aviation Administration
FEDLOG	Federal logistics
FM	field manual
FORSCOM	U.S. Army Forces Command
FSC	federal supply classification
GCSS-ARMY	Global Command Support System-Army
HAZMAT	hazardous material
HGU	head gear unit
IHADSS	intgrated helmet and display sight system
IL	identification list
ISOPREP	isolated personnel report
JP	joint publication
LIDB	logistics integrated database
LIN	line item number
LOGSA	U.S. Army Logistics Support Activity
LPU	life preserver unit
LSE	logistics support element
MAC	maintenance allocation chart
METS	modular egress training simulator
MOPP	mission orienteted protective posture
MOS	military occupational speciality
MTOE	modification table of organization and equipment
MWO	modification work order
NAVAIR	Naval Air
NCO	noncommissioned officer
NSN	national stock number
OCIE	organizational clothing and individual equipment
PBO	property book officer
PC	pilot-in-command
PCE	protective clothing and equipment
PLL	prescribed load list
PM	product manager
PMCS	preventive maintenance checks and services
POL	petroleum, oil, and lubricants
PRC	personal radio communicator
PTT	push-to-talk
QASAS	quality assurance specialist (ammunition surveillance)
S2	intelligence officer
S3	operations officer
S4	logistics officer

SAMS	Standard Army Maintenance System
SAMS-E	Standard Army Maintenance System-Enhanced
SAMS-1	Standard Army Maintenance System-Level 1
SAMS-2	Standard Army Maintenance System-Level 2
SARSS	Standard Army Retail Supply System
SARSS-1	Standard Army Retail Supply System-Level 1
SARSS-2A/C	Standard Army Retail Supply System-Level 2A/C
SB	supply bulletin
SC	supply catalog
SERE	survival, evasion, resistance, and escape
SF	standard form
SOP	standing operating procedure
SPINS	special instructions
SSA	supply support activity
SWET	shallow water egress trainer
TB	technical bulletin
TC	training circular
TDA	table of distribution and allowances
TMDE	test, measurement, and diagnostic equipment
TM	technical manual
TO	technical order
TPL	thermal plastic liner
TRADOC	U.S. Army Training and Doctrine Command
TS	test set
TTP	tactics, techniques, and procedures
UDR	universal data repository
ULLS	Unit Level Logistics System
ULLS-A	Unit Level Logistics System-Aviation
ULLS-G	Unit Level Logistics System-Ground
ULLS-S4	Unit Level Logistics System-Supply
UND	urgency of need designator
USAARL	U.S. Army Aeromedical Research Laboratory
USACRC	U.S. Army Combat Readiness/Safety Center
USAF	U.S. Air Force

This page intentionally left blank.

References

The following publications provide additional information on topics discussed in this TC. Most Army publications are available online at http://www.apd.army.mil/. Most joint publications are available online at http://www.dtic.mil/doctrine/doctrine.htm.

SOURCES USED

These sources are quoted or paraphrased within this publication.

AR 95-1. *Flight Regulations*. 12 November 2008.

AR 190-11. *Physical Security of Arms, Ammunition, and Explosives*. 15 November 2006.

AR 710-2. *Supply Policy Below the National Level*. 28 March 2008.

AR 735-5. *Policies and Procedures for Property Accountability*. 28 February 2005.

AR 740-1. *Storage and Supply Activity Operations*. 26 August 2008.

DA Pam 25-30. *Consolidated Index of Army Publications and Blank Forms*. 14 July 2009.

DA Pam 25-33. *User's Guide for Army Publications and Forms*. 15 September 1996.

DA Pam 710-2-1. *Using Unit Supply System (Manual Procedures)*. 31 December 1997.

DA Pam 710-2-2. *Supply Support Activity Supply System: Manual Procedures*. 30 September 1998.

DOCUMENTS NEEDED

These documents must be available to intended users of this publication. DA Forms are available on the APD website (www.apd.army.mil). DD Forms are available on the OSD website (www.dtic mil/whs/directives/infomgt/forms/formsprogram.htm).

DA Form 581. *Request for Issue and Turn-In of Ammunition*.

DA Form 581-1. *Request for Issue and Turn-In of Ammunition Continuation Sheet*.

DA Form 1687. *Notice of Delegation of Authority-Receipt for Supplies*.

DA Form 2028. *Recommended Changes to Publications and Blank Forms*.

DA Form 2062. *Hand Receipt/Annex Number*.

DA Form 2064. *Document Register for Supply Actions*.

DA Form 2408-18. *Equipment Inspection List*.

DA Form 2408-22. *Helmet and Oxygen Mask/Connector Inspection Record*.

DA Form 2408-23. *Survival Radio/Emergency Locator Transmitter Inspection Record*.

DA Form 2408-24. *Survival Kit Inspection and Maintenance Record*.

DA Form 2408-25. *Mesh Net Survival Vest Inspection Record*.

DA Form 2408-26. *Life Preserver Inspection Record*.

DA Form 2408-27. *Life Preserver Data*.

DA Form 2765-1. *Request for Issue or Turn-In*.

DA Form 3022-R. *Army Depot Surveillance Record*. (LRA)

DA Form 3161. *Request for Issue or Turn-In*.

DA Form 3749. *Equipment Receipt*.

DA Form 4604. *Security Construction Statement*.

DA Form 5513. *Key Control Register and Inventory*.

DD Form 448. *Military Interdepartmental Purchase Request*.

DD Form 1150. *Request for Issue or Turn-In*.

DD Form 1348-1A. *Issue Release/Receipt Document*.

DD Form 1348-6. *DOD Single Line Item Requisition System Document(Manual- Long Form).*

DD Form 1574. *Serviceable Tag-Materiel.*

DD Form 1577. *Unserviceable (Condemned) Tag-Materiel.*

DD Form 1577-2. *Unserviceable (Reparable) Tag-Materiel.*

DD Form 1750. *Packing List.*

DD Form 1833. *Isolated Personnel Report (ISOPREP).*

SF 364. *Report of Discrepancy (ROD).*

SF 368. *Product Quality Deficiency Report.*

READINGS RECOMMENDED

These sources contain relevant supplemental information.

Air Force Regulation 64-4V1. *Survival Training.* 1 July 1985.

AR 25-400-2. *The Army Records Information Management System (ARIMS).* 2 October 2007.

AR 40-61. *Medical Logistics Policies.* 28 January 2005.

AR 95-20. *Contractor's Flight and Ground Operations.* 1 March 2007.

AR 190-13. *The Army Physical Security Program.* 30 September 1993.

AR 190-51. *Security of Unclassified Army Property (Sensitive and Nonsensitive).* 30 September 1993.

AR 350-30. *Code of Conduct/Survival, Evasion, Resistance, and Escape (SERE) Training.*
10 December 1985.

AR 350-50. *Combat Training Center Program.* 24 January 2003.

AR 385-10. *The Army Safety Program.* 23 August 2007.

AR 525-90. *Combat Search and Rescue Procedures.* 25 February 1985.

AR 600-106. *Flying Status for Nonrated Army Aviation Personnel.* 8 December 1998.

AR 702-6. *Ammunition Stockpile Reliability Program.* 23 June 2009.

AR 710-1. *Centralized Inventory Management of the Army Supply System.* 20 September 2007.

AR 725-50. *Requisition, Receipt, and Issue System.* 15 November 1995.

AR 735-11-2. *Reporting of Supply Discrepancies.* 6 August 2001.

ATTP 3-04.7 (FM 3-04.500). *Army Aviation Maintenance.* 23 August 2006.

CTA 8-100. *Army Medical Department Expendable/Durable Items.* 17 December 2004.

CTA 50-900. *Clothing and Individual Equipment.* 1 September 1994.

CTA 50-909. *Field and Garrison Furnishings and Equipment.* 1 August 1993.

DA Pam 25-40. *Army Publishing: Action Officers Guide.* 7 November 2006.

DA Pam 385-40. *Army Accident Investigations and Reporting.* 6 March 2009.

DA Pam 385-64. *Ammunition and Explosives Safety Standards.* 15 December 1999.

DA Pam 385-90. *Army Aviation Accident Prevention.* 28 August 2007.

DA Pam 611-21. *Military Occupational Classification and Structure.* 22 January 2007.

DA Pam 708-2. *Cataloging and Supply Management Data Procedures for the Army Central Logistics Data Bank.* 23 May 2008.

DA Pam 738-751. *Functional Users Manual for the Army Maintenance Management System-- (TAMMS-A).* 15 March 1999.

FM 3-05.70. *Survival.* 17 May 2002.

FM 4-01.011. *Unit Movement Operations.* 31 October 2002.

FM 5-19. *Composite Risk Management.* 21 August 2006.

FM 55-1. *Transportation Operations.* 3 October 1995.

FM 55-30. *Army Motor Transport Units and Operations.* 27 June 1997.

FORSCOM Regulation 55-1. *Unit Movement Planning.* 1 June 2006.

FORSCOM Regulation 55-2. *Unit Movement Data Reporting and Systems Administration.* 31 October 1997.

JP 3-50. *Personnel Recovery.* 5 January 2007.

SB 11-6. *Communications Electronics Batteries Supply and Management Data.* 1 June 2001.

SB 742-1. *Inspection of Supplies and Equipment Ammunition Surveillance Procedures.* 1 September 2008.

TB 55-46-1. *Standard Characteristics (Dimensions, Weight, and Cube) for Transportability of Military Vehicles and Other Outsize/Overweight Equipment (in TOE Line Item Number Sequence).* 19 March 2009.

TC 1-210. *Aircrew Training Program Commander's Guide to Individual, Crew, and Collective Training.* 20 June 2006.

TC 21-3. *Soldier's Handbook for Individual Operations and Survival in Cold-Weather Areas.* 17 March 1986.

TC 21-21. *Water Survival Training.* 25 June 1991.

TM 1-1500-204-23-1. *Aviation Unit Maintenance (AVUM) and Aviation Intermediate Maintenance (AVIM) Manual for General Aircraft Maintenance (General Maintenance and Practices) Volume 1.* 31 July 1992.

TM 1-1500-344-23-1. *Cleaning and Corrosion Control, Volume 1.* 1 March 2005.

TM 1-8415-215-12&P. *Operator's and Aviation Unit Maintenance Manual Including Repair Parts and Special Tools List for Helmet, Flyer's; SPH-4B (NSN 8415-01-308-5359) (Regular) (8415-01-308-5360) (Extra Large) (NG) (AR).* 15 January 1993.

TM 9-1270-233-23&P. *Aviation Unit and Intermediate Maintenance Manual (Including Repair Parts and Special Tools List) for Helmet Unit, Integrated (NSN 1270-01-295-6255) (Medium), (1270-01-298-3544)(Large), and (1270-01-263-2545) (X-Large).* 15 December 1988.

TM 11-5820-1037-13&P. *Operator's Unit, and Intermediate Maintenance (Repair Parts and Special Tools List) for Radio Set AN/PRC-112 (NSN 5820-01-279-5450) (EIC: JBG) Program Loader KY 913/PRC-112 (NSN 7025-01-279-5308).* 15 July 2005.

TM 11-5820-1049-12. *Operator's and Aviation Unit Maintenance Manual for Radio Set AN/PRC-90-2 (NSN 5820-01-238-6603).* 15 August 1990.

TM 38-250. *Preparing Hazardous Materials for Military Air Shipments.* 15 April 2007.

TM 43-0001-37. *Army Ammunition Data Sheets for Military Pyrotechnics (Federal Supply Class 1370).* 6 January 1994.

TM 55-1520-400-14. *Transportability Guidance Marine Transport of US Army Helicopters.* 28 April 1978.

TM 55-1680-317-23&P. *Aviation Unit and Aviation Intermediate Maintenance Manual with Repair Parts and Special Tools List for Army Aircraft Survival Kits.* 26 March 1987.

TM 55-1680-322-12. *Operation and Service: Distress Marker Light, Part No. ACR/MS-2000M (NSN 6230-01-411-8535) and Part No. SDU-5/E (NSN 6230-00-067-5209).* 31 August 2000.

TM 750-244-1-2. *Procedures for the Destruction of Life Support Equipment to Prevent Enemy Use.* 22 October 1971.

TRADOC Regulation 385-2. *U.S. Army Training and Doctrine Command Safety Program.* 23 January 2009.

WEBSITES RECOMMENDED

Air Force Publications: https://www.my.af.mil/faf/FAF/fafHome.jsp

ARMS Checklist: https://www.us.army.mil/suite/page/592726

ARMS Commander's Guide: https://www.us.army.mil/suite/page/592726

Army Automated Life Support Management System: http://ArmyALSMS.com

Army Institute for Professional Development-Correspondence:
   http://www.atsc.army mil/accp/aipdnew.asp

Army Publishing Directorate: http://www.apd.army mil/

Defense Logistics Information Service: http://www.dlis.dla.mil/

Defense Prisoner of War/Missing Personnel Office: http://www.dtic mil/dpmo/

Defense Supply Center-Maps Facility: http://www.dscr.dla.mil/rmf/products/aero/aero.htm

Defense Supply Center Philadelphia: www.dscp.dla mil/

Defense Imagery: http://www.defenseimagery.mil/index html

Electronic Forms: http://www.apd.army mil

General Dennis J. Reimer Training and Doctrine Digital Library: http://www.adtdl.army mil/

Joint Services Air Land Sea Applications Center: http://www.alsa.mil

Joint Services Electronic Library: http://www.dtic.mil/doctrine/

Naval Education and Training Command: https://www netc navy mil/

Naval Operational Medicine Institute: http://www.med navy mil/Pages/Default.aspx

U.S. Navy Publications: http://doni.daps.dla.mil/default.aspx

PM-Air Warrior: https://airwarrior.redstone.army mil

Tracker 2.0: https://airwarrior.redstone.army mil/default.asp

U.S. Air Force Rescue Coordination Center: http://www.1af.acc.af mil/units/afrcc/

U.S. Army Logistics Support Activity: https://www.logsa.army.mil

U.S. Army Medical Department: http://www.armymedicine.army.mil

U.S. Navy SERE School: https://www netc.navy.mil/centers/csf/

Index

This page intentionally left blank.

By Order of the Secretary of the Army:

GEORGE W. CASEY, JR.
General, United States Army
Chief of Staff

Official:

JOYCE E. MORROW
Administrative Assistant to the
Secretary of the Army
0926007

DISTRIBUTION:

Active Army, Army National Guard, and U.S. Army Reserve: To be distributed in accordance with the initial distribution number (IDN) 110730, requirements for TC 3-04.72.

www.ingramcontent.com/pod-product-compliance
Lightning Source LLC
Chambersburg PA
CBHW081650270326
41933CB00018B/3423